Zoo Tiere
Malbuch

Coloring Pages for Kids

Coloring Pages for Kids
An imprint of Ciparum LLC

Zoo Tiere Malbuch
© 2017 Ciparum LLC
All rights reserved.
ISBN-10:1-63589-435-2
ISBN-13:978-1-63589-435-6

Coloring Pages for Kids

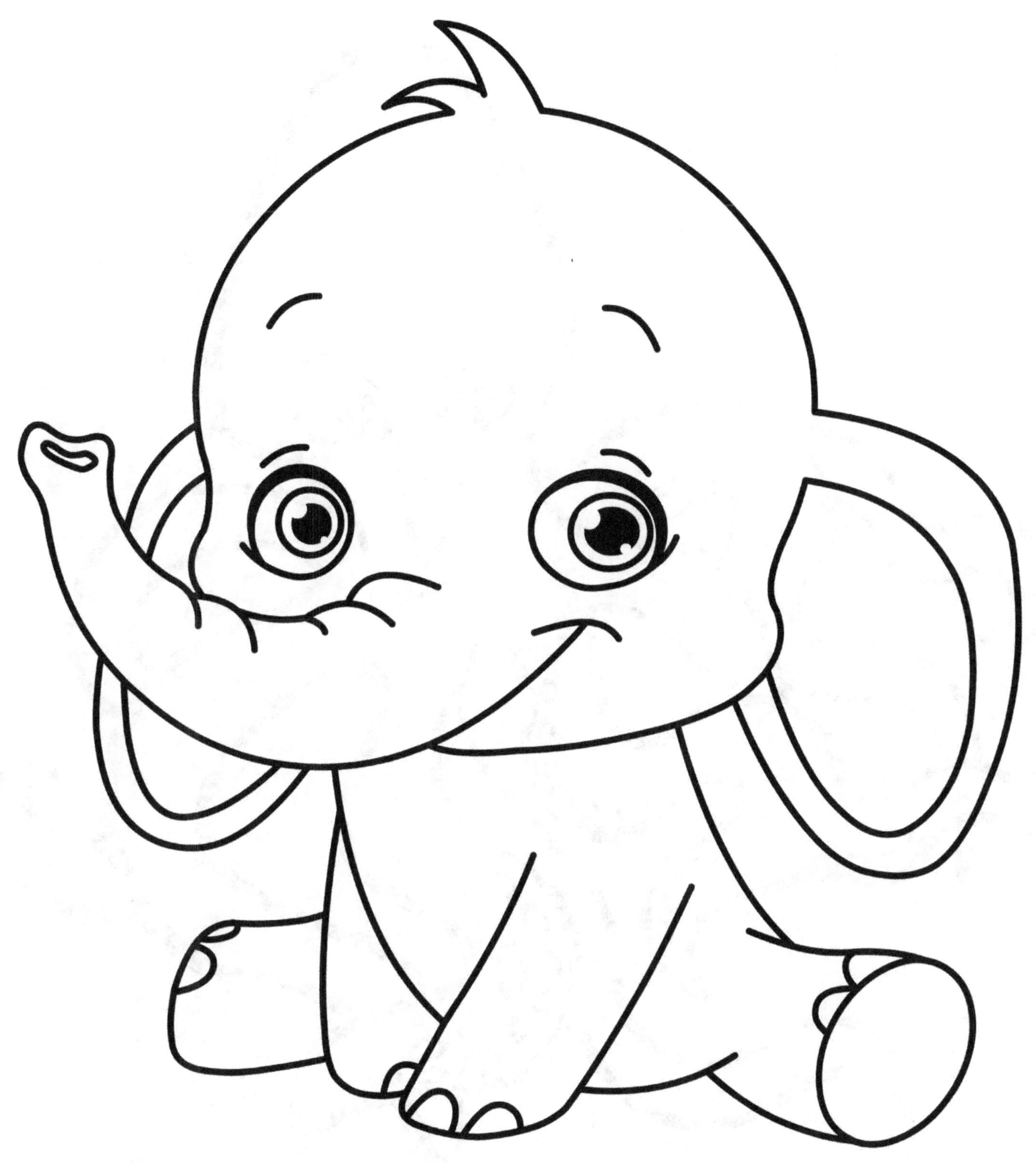

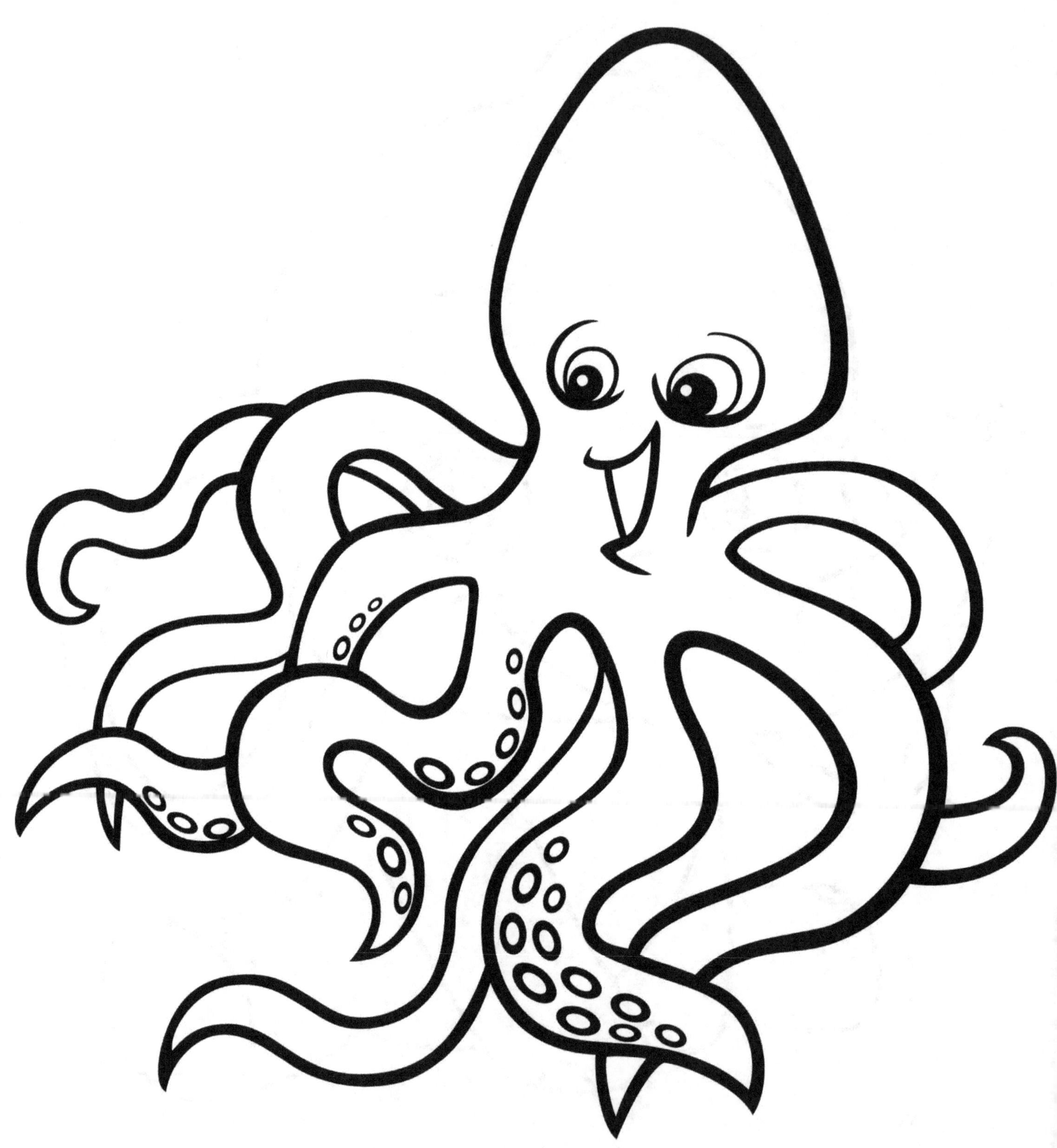

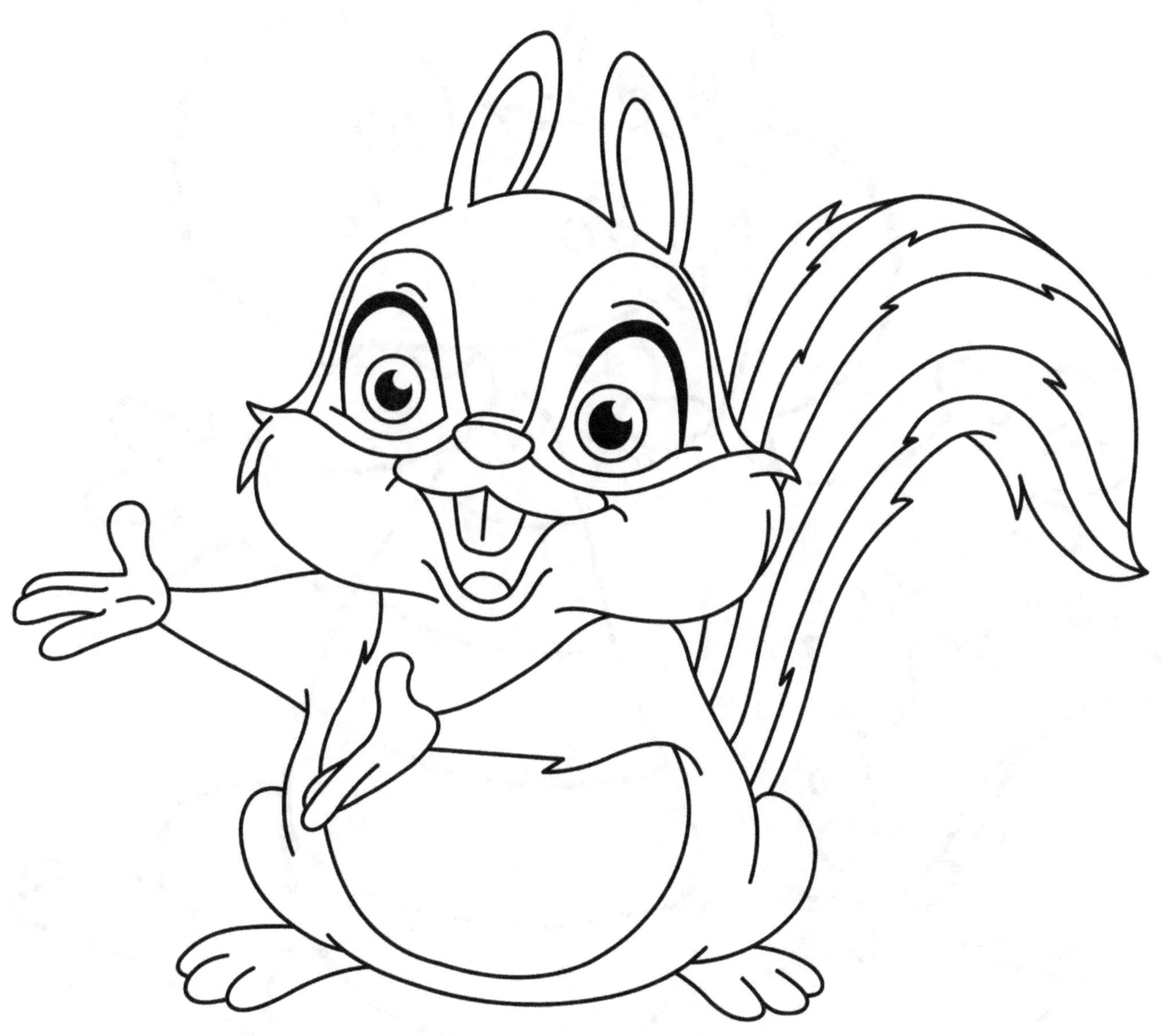

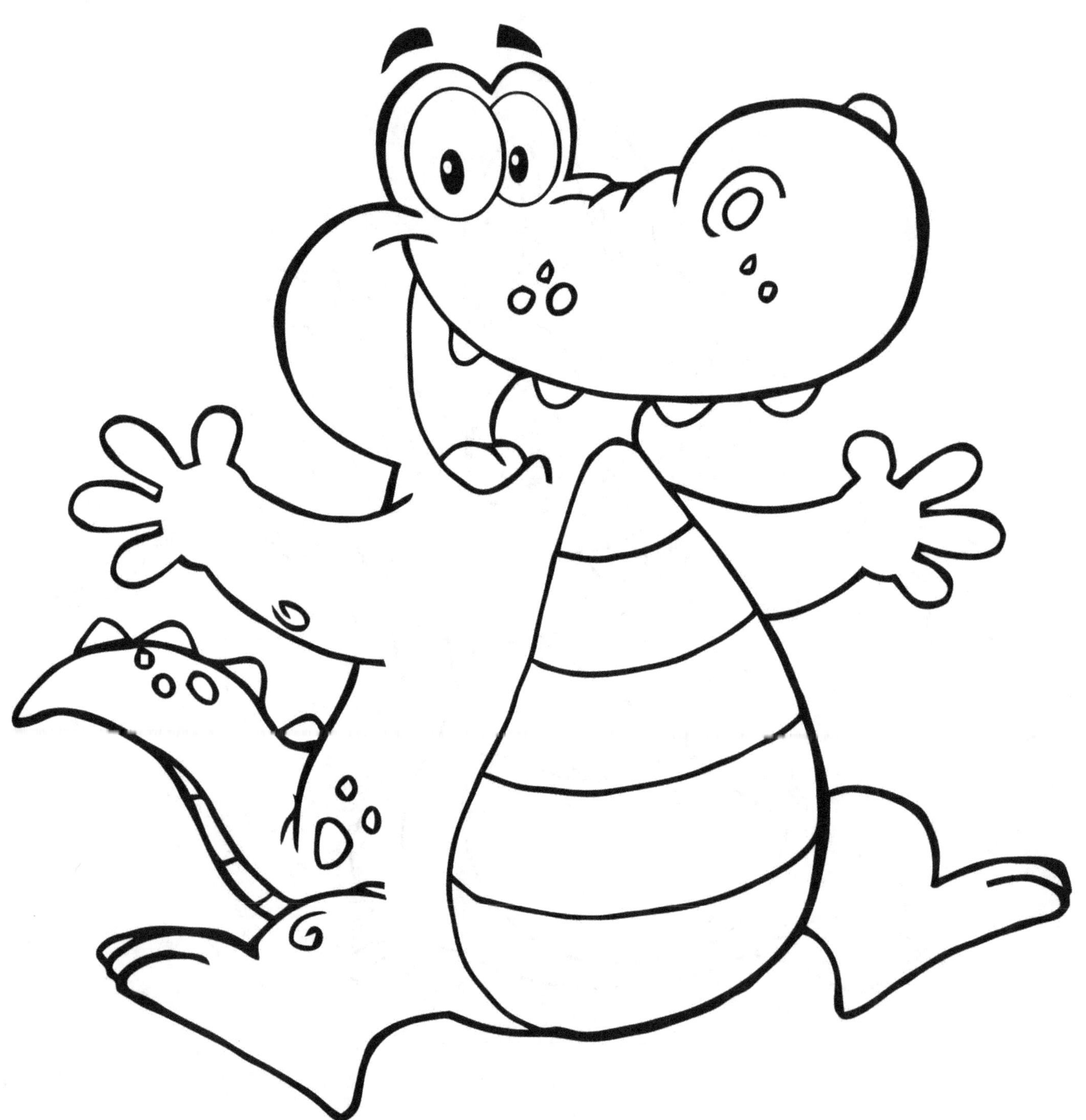

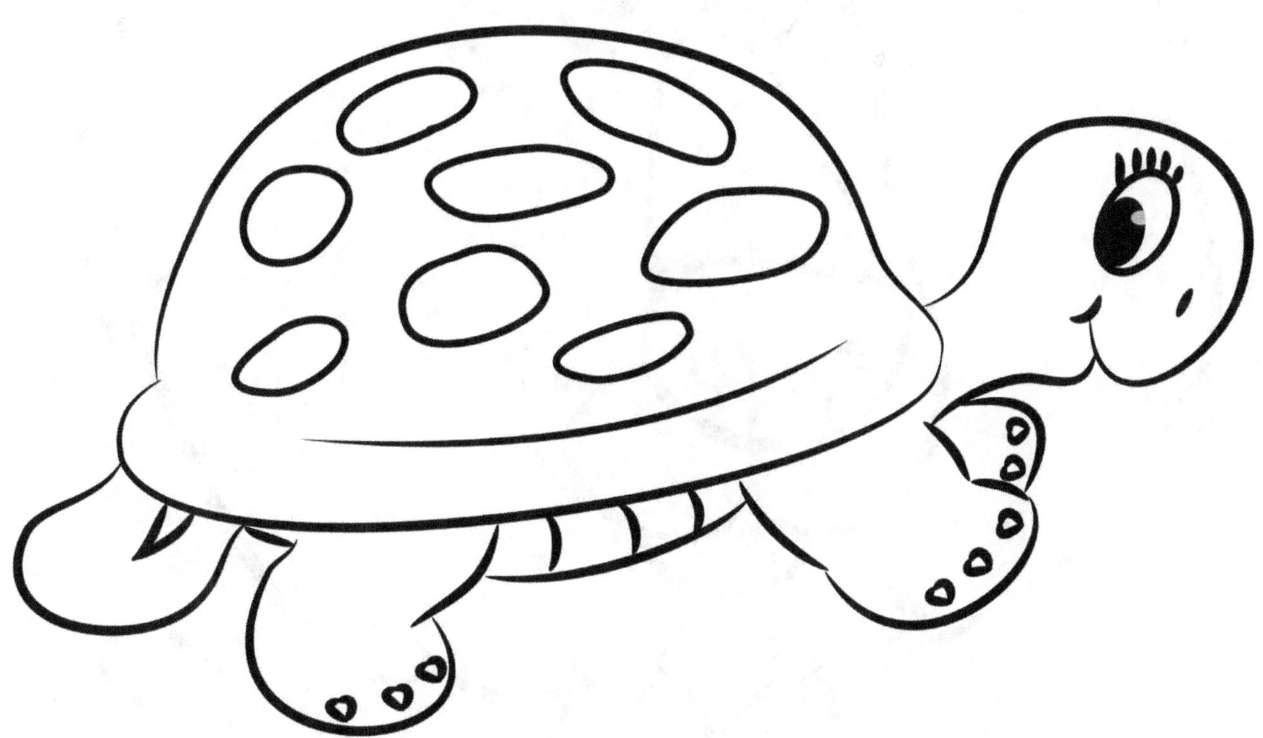

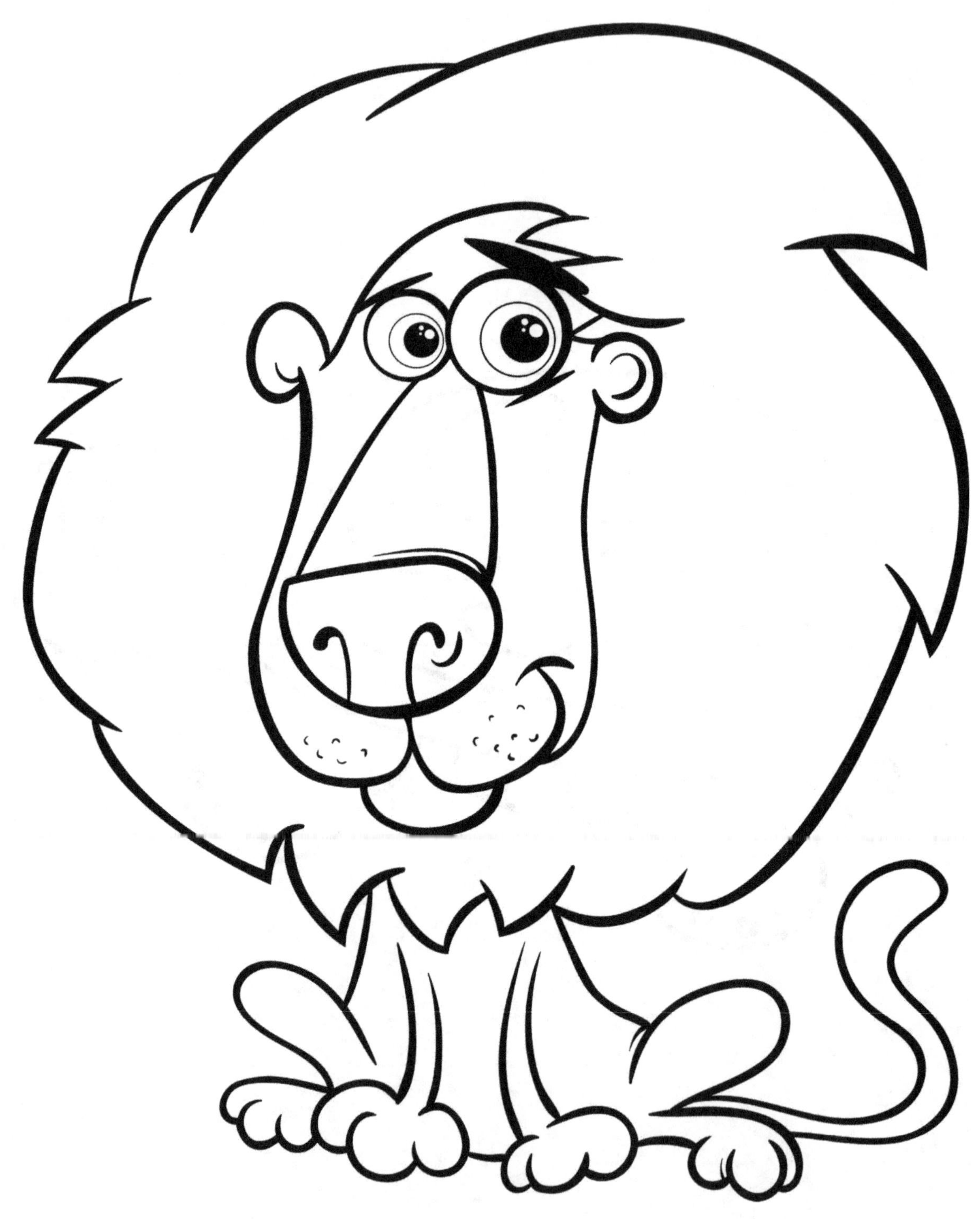

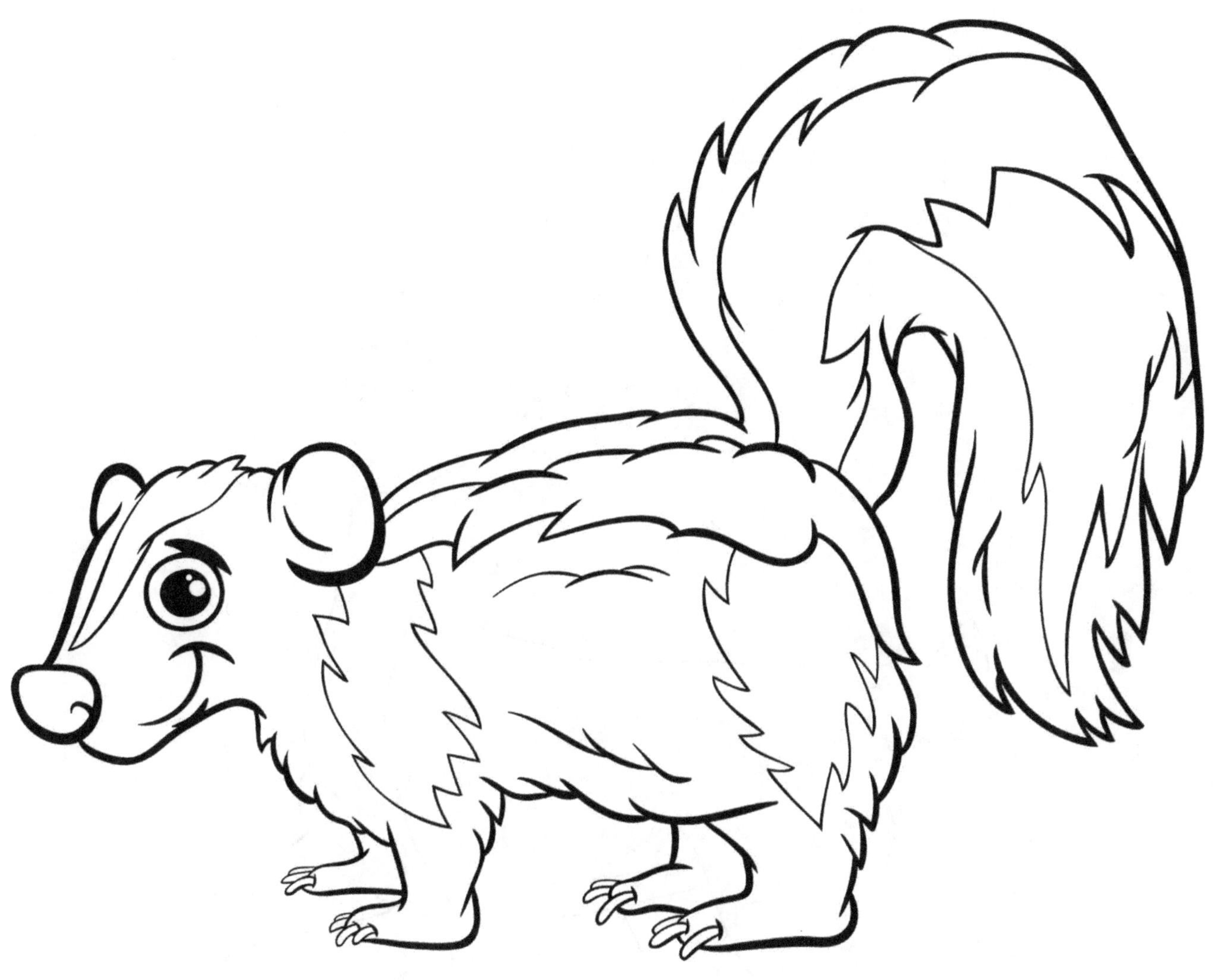

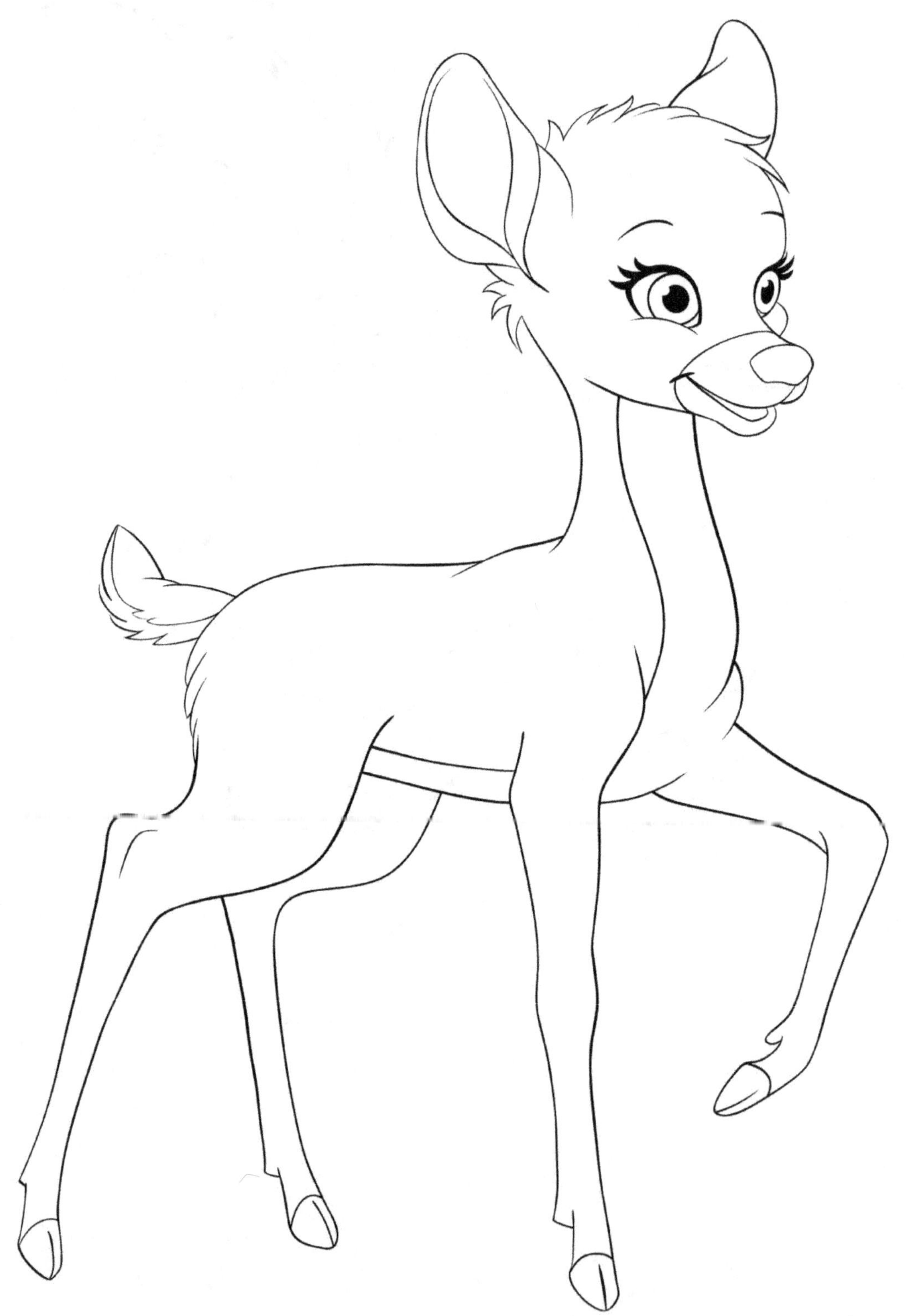

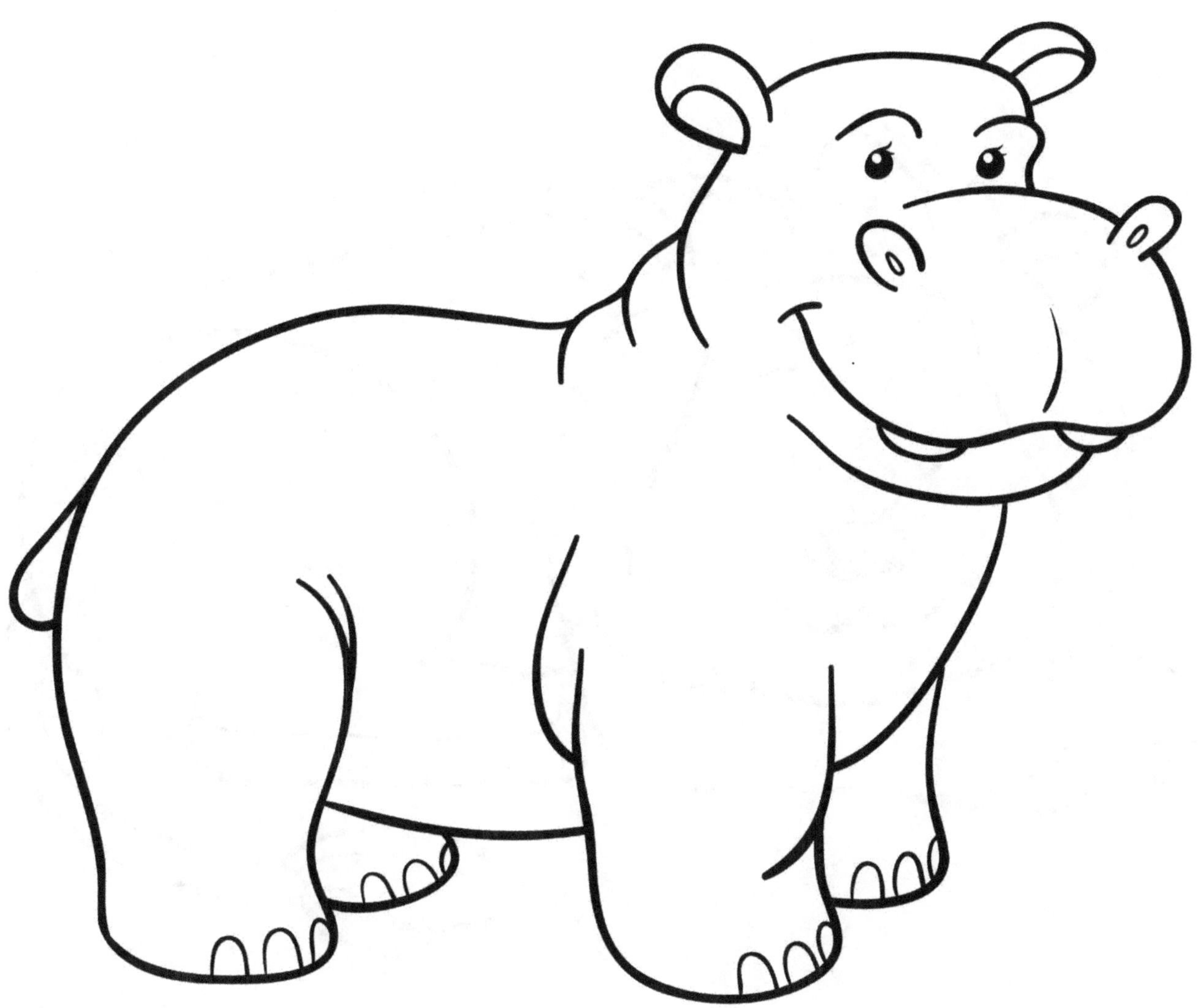

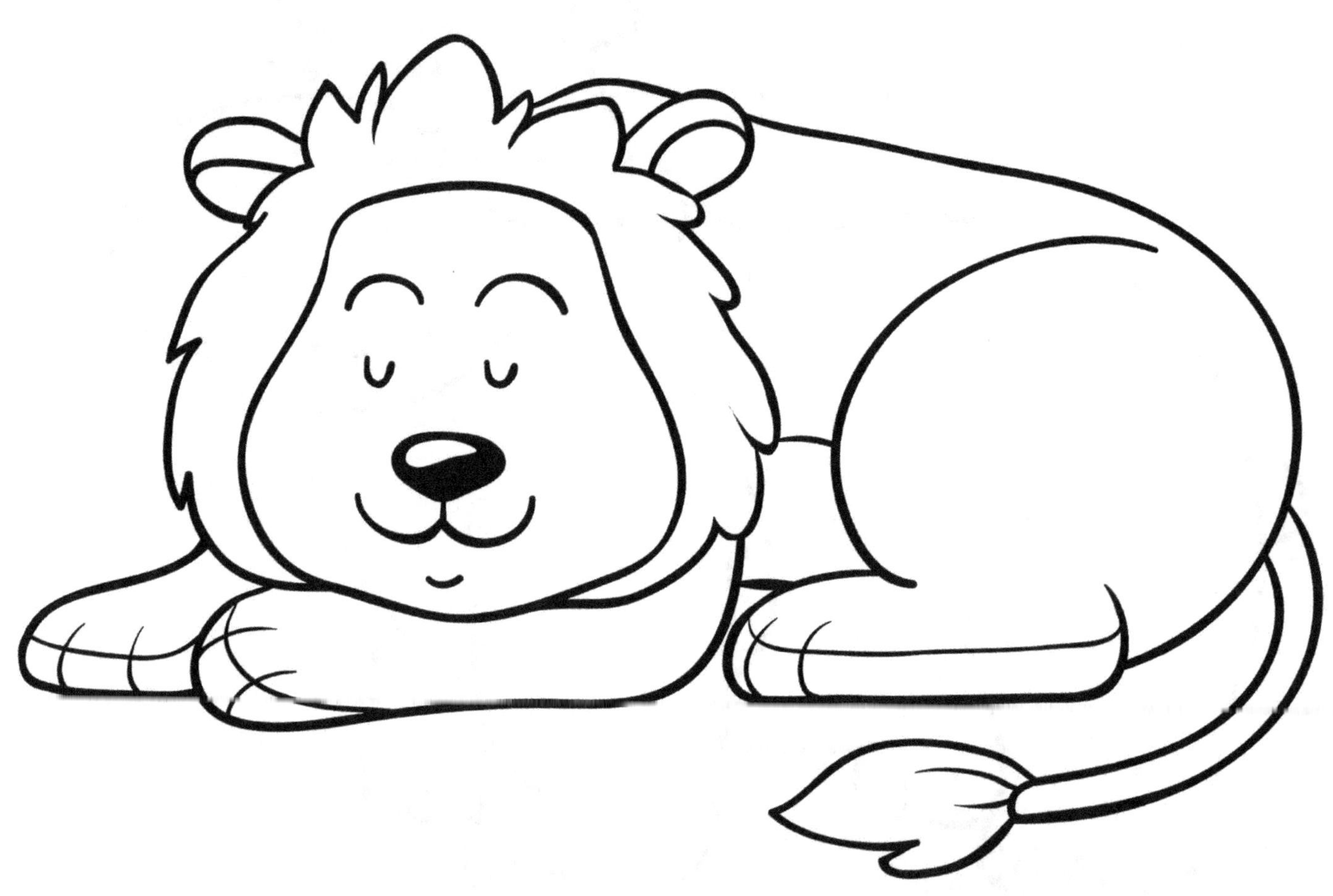

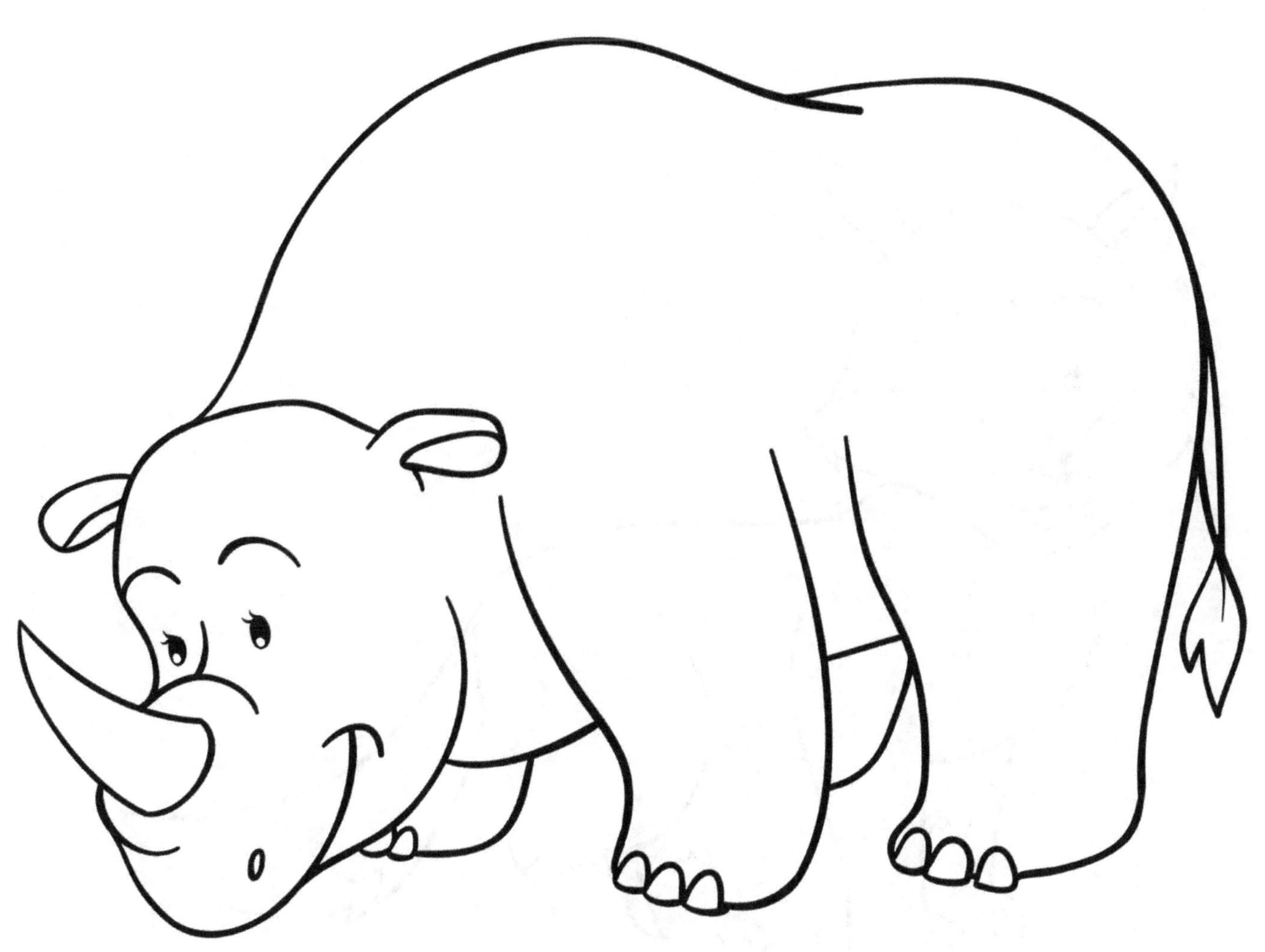

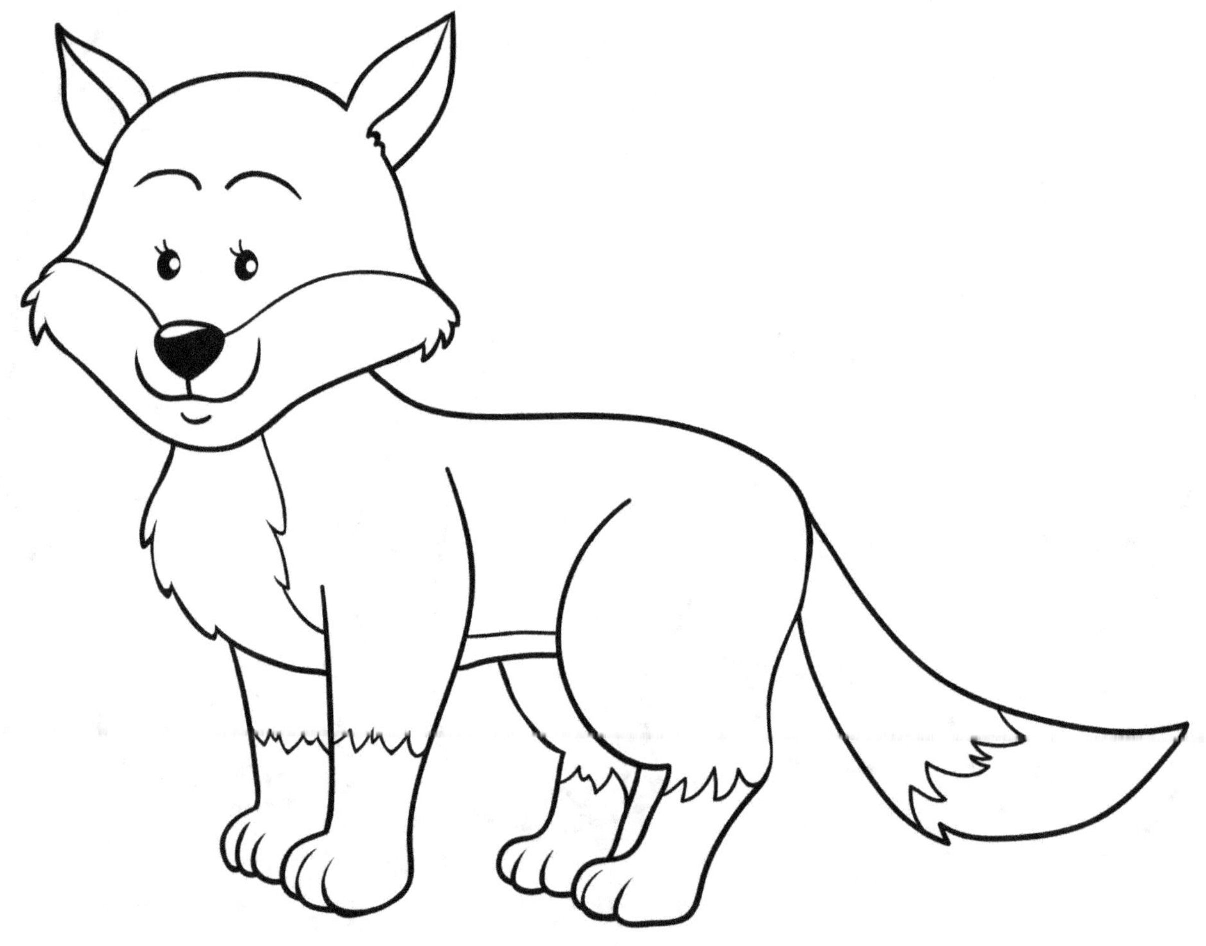

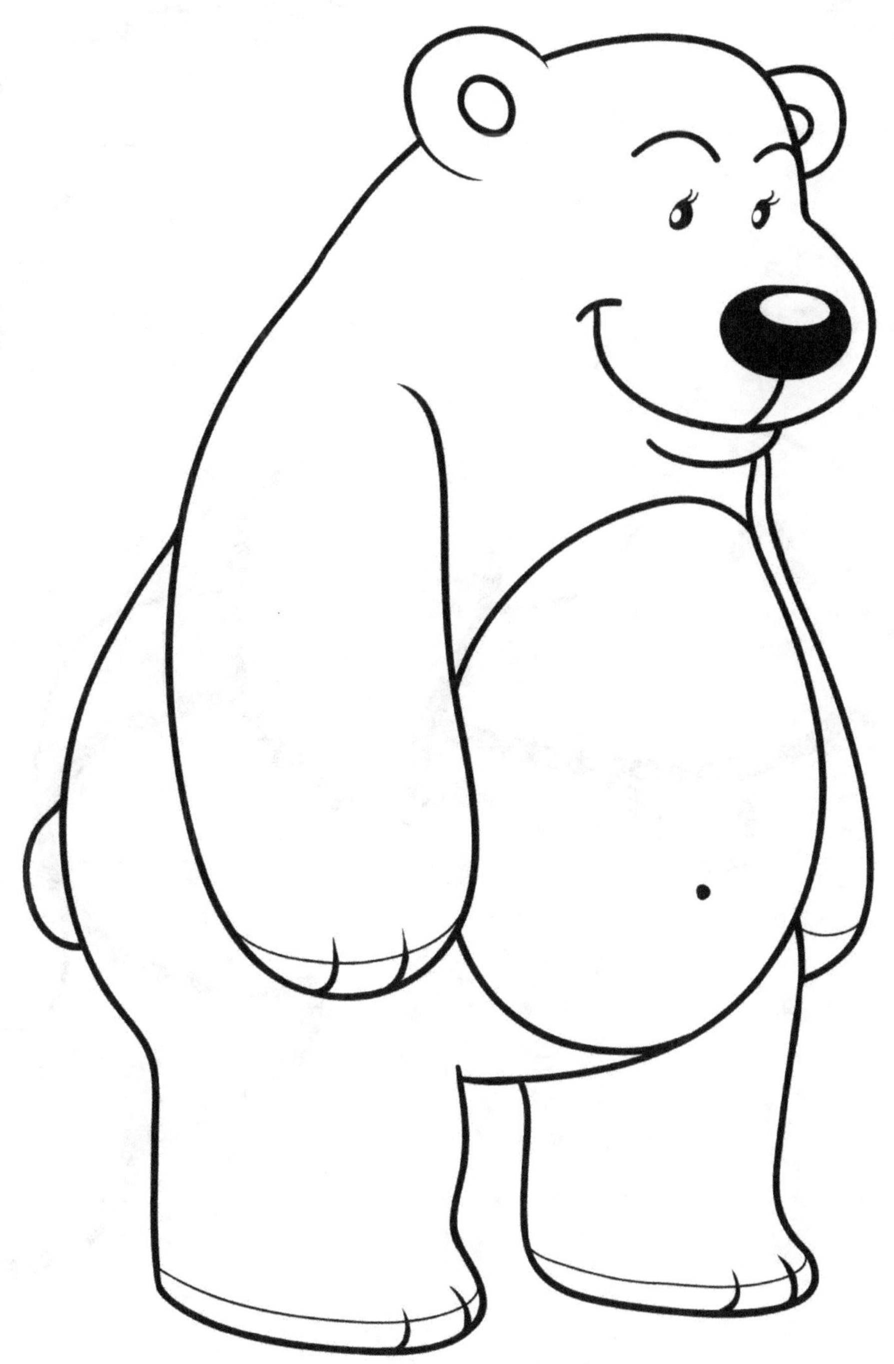

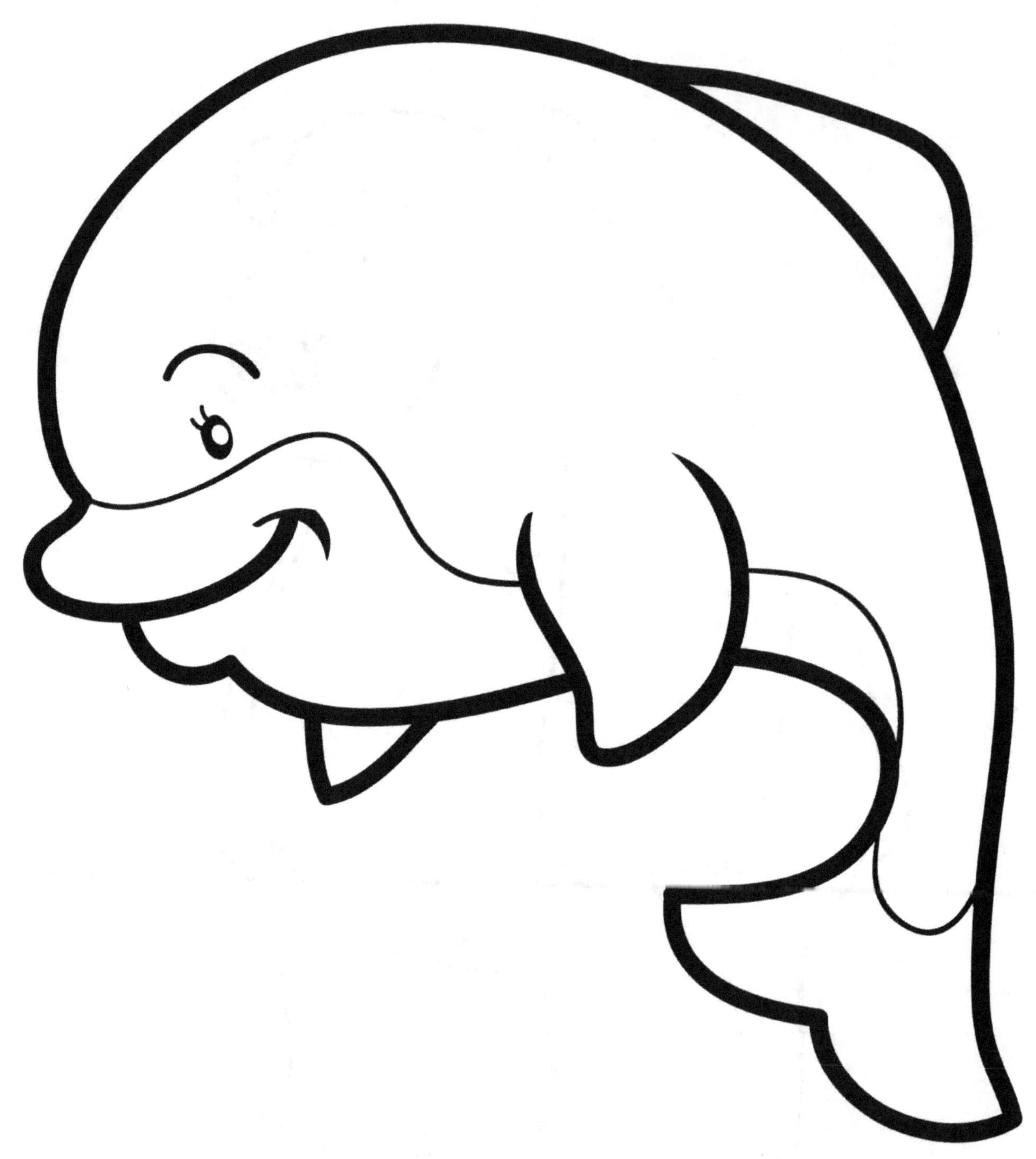

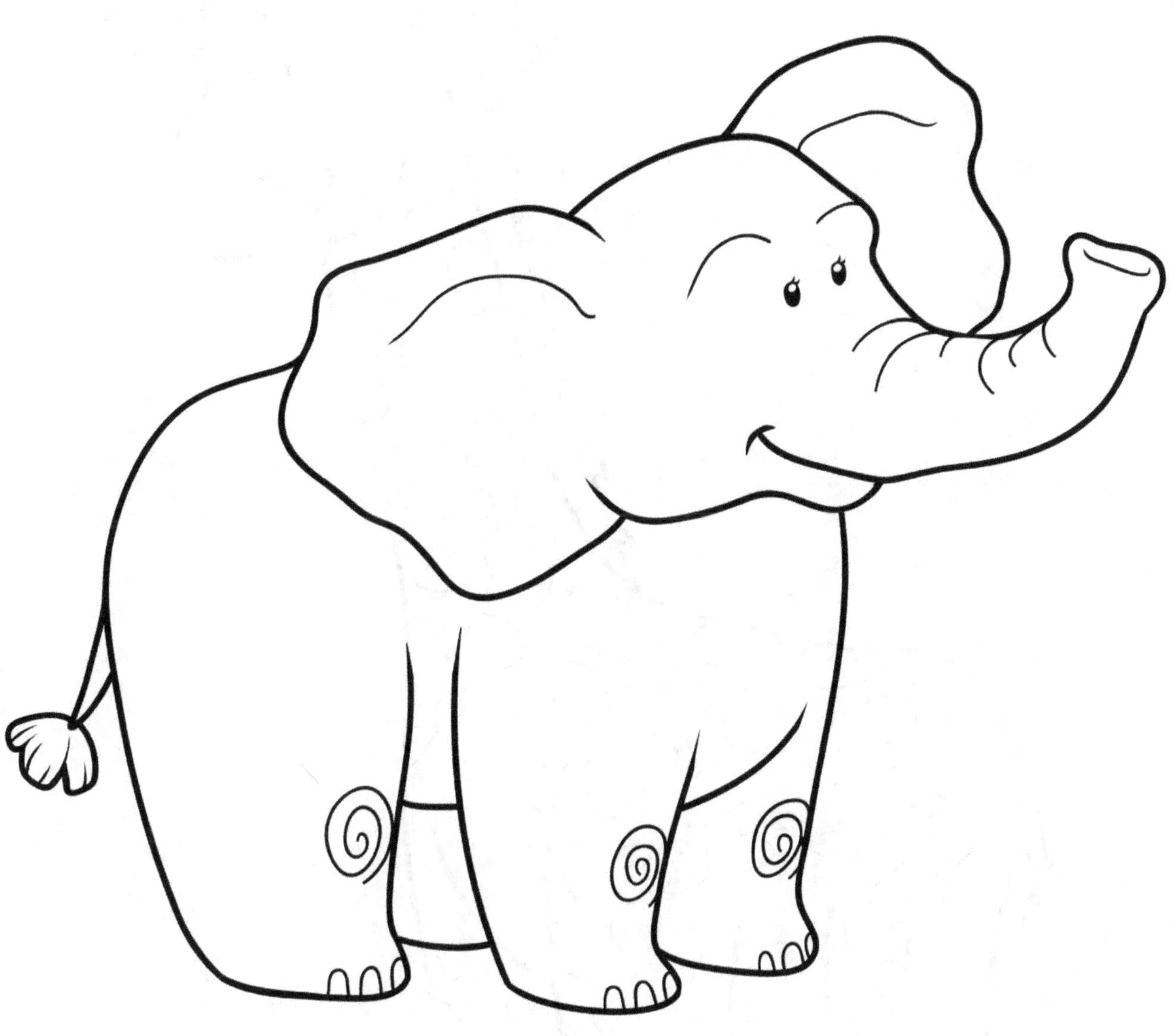

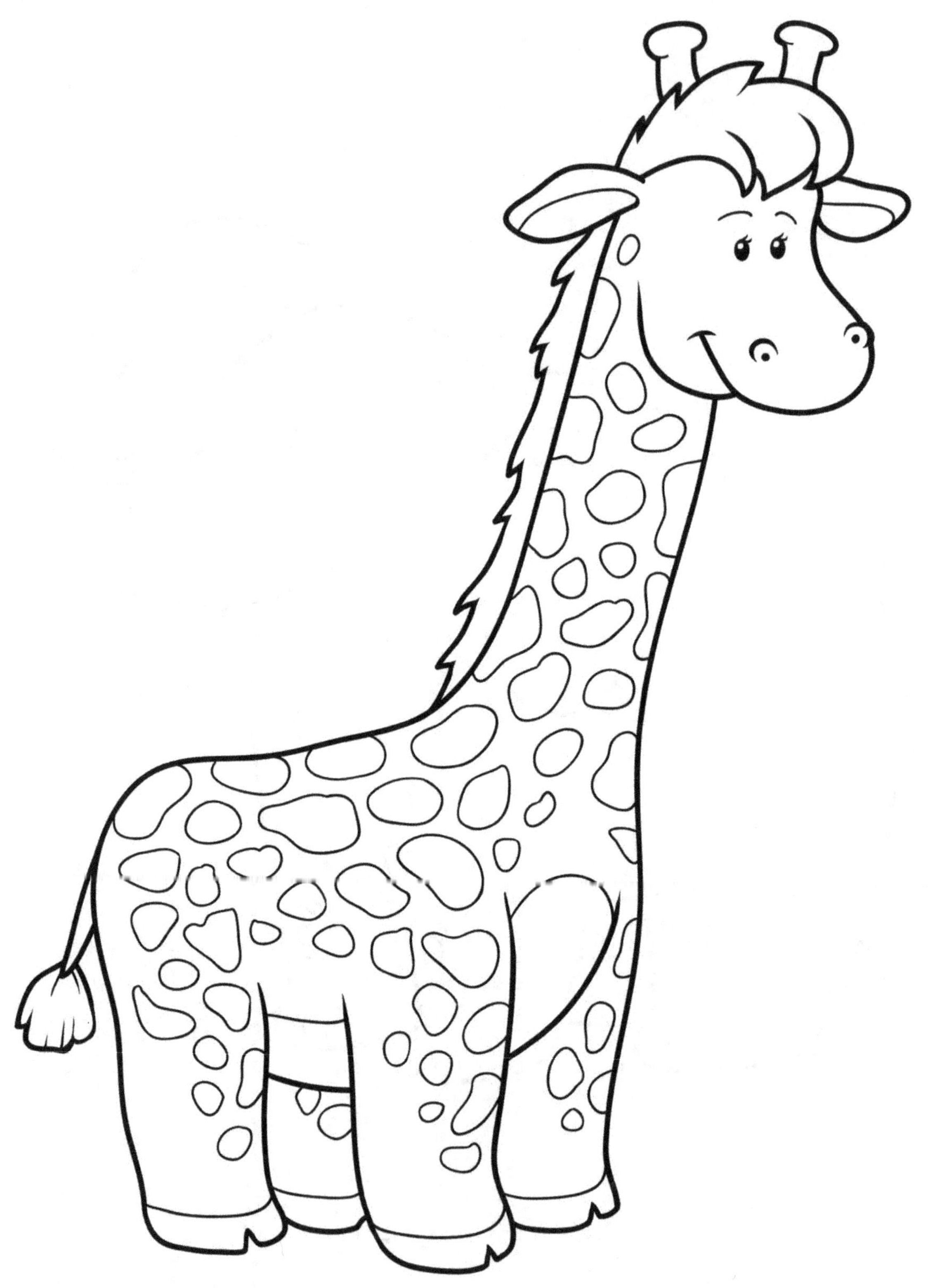

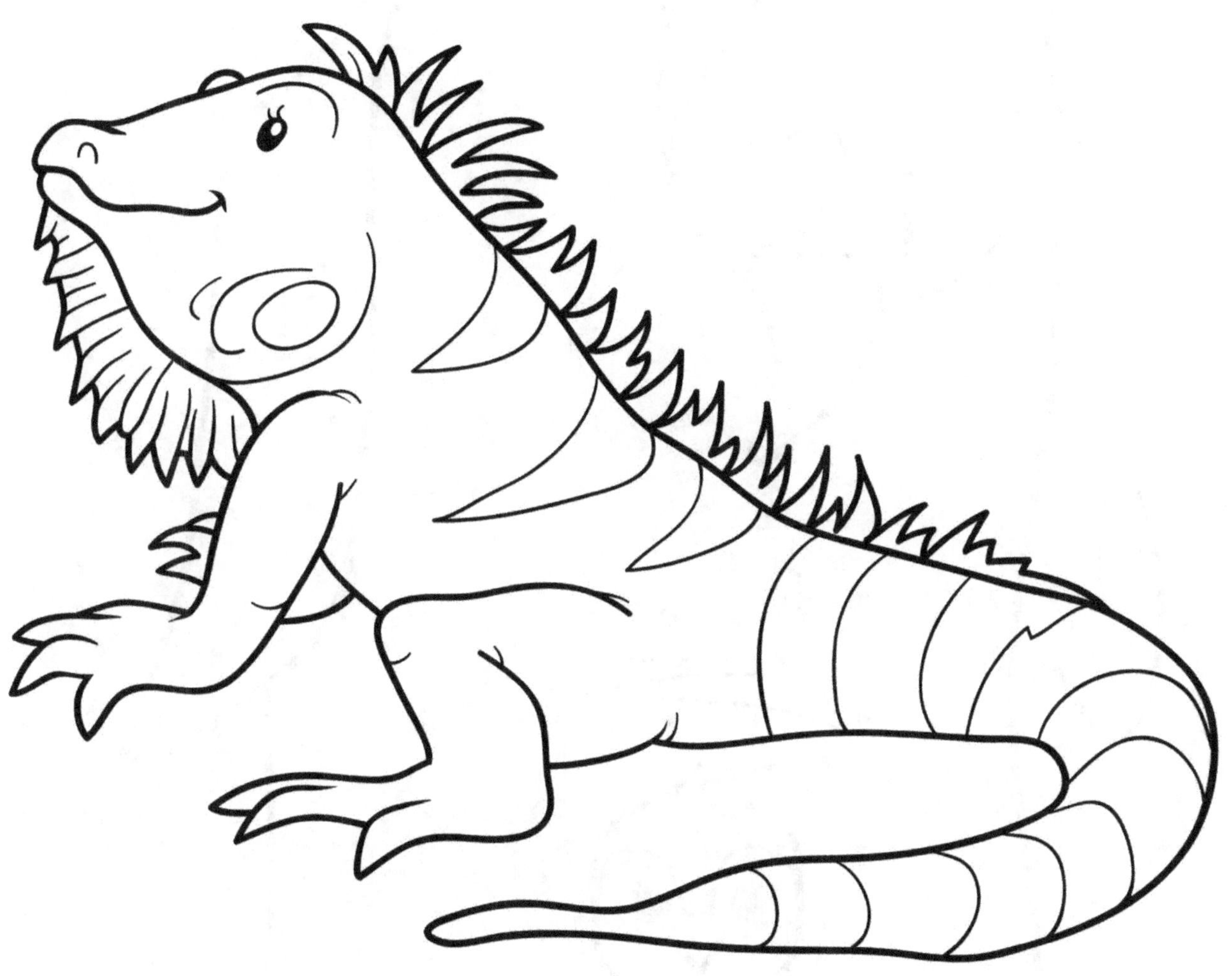

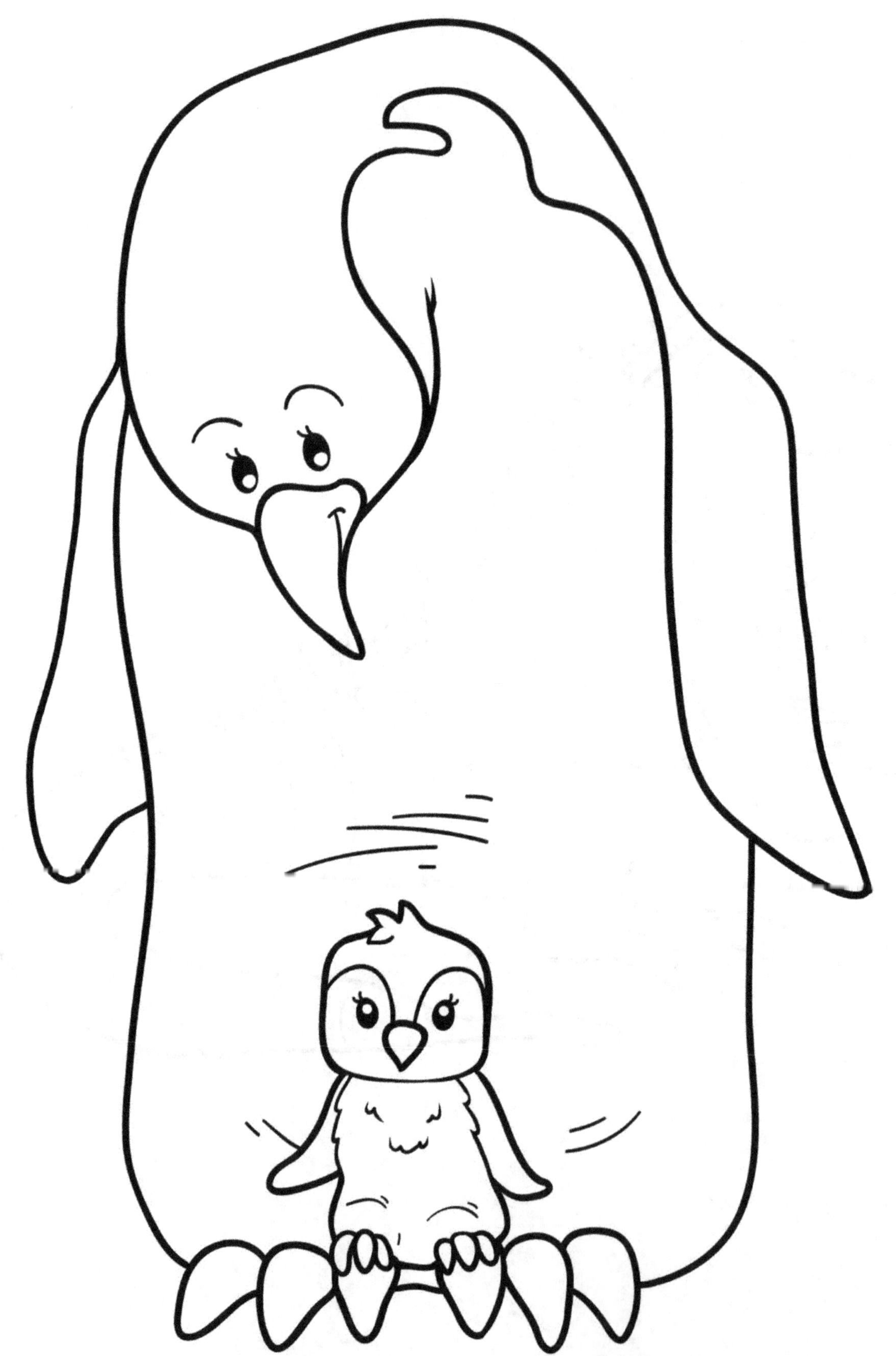

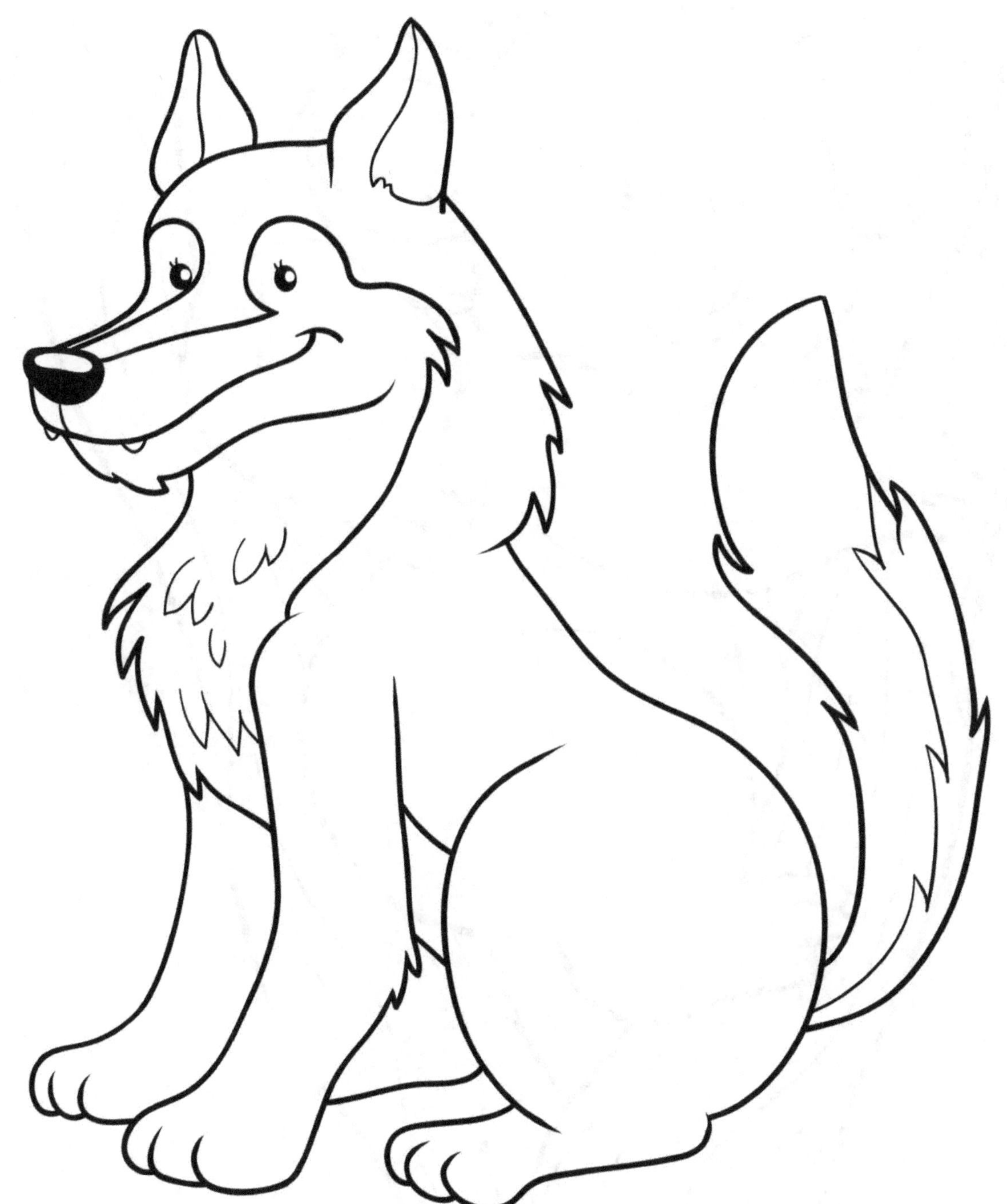

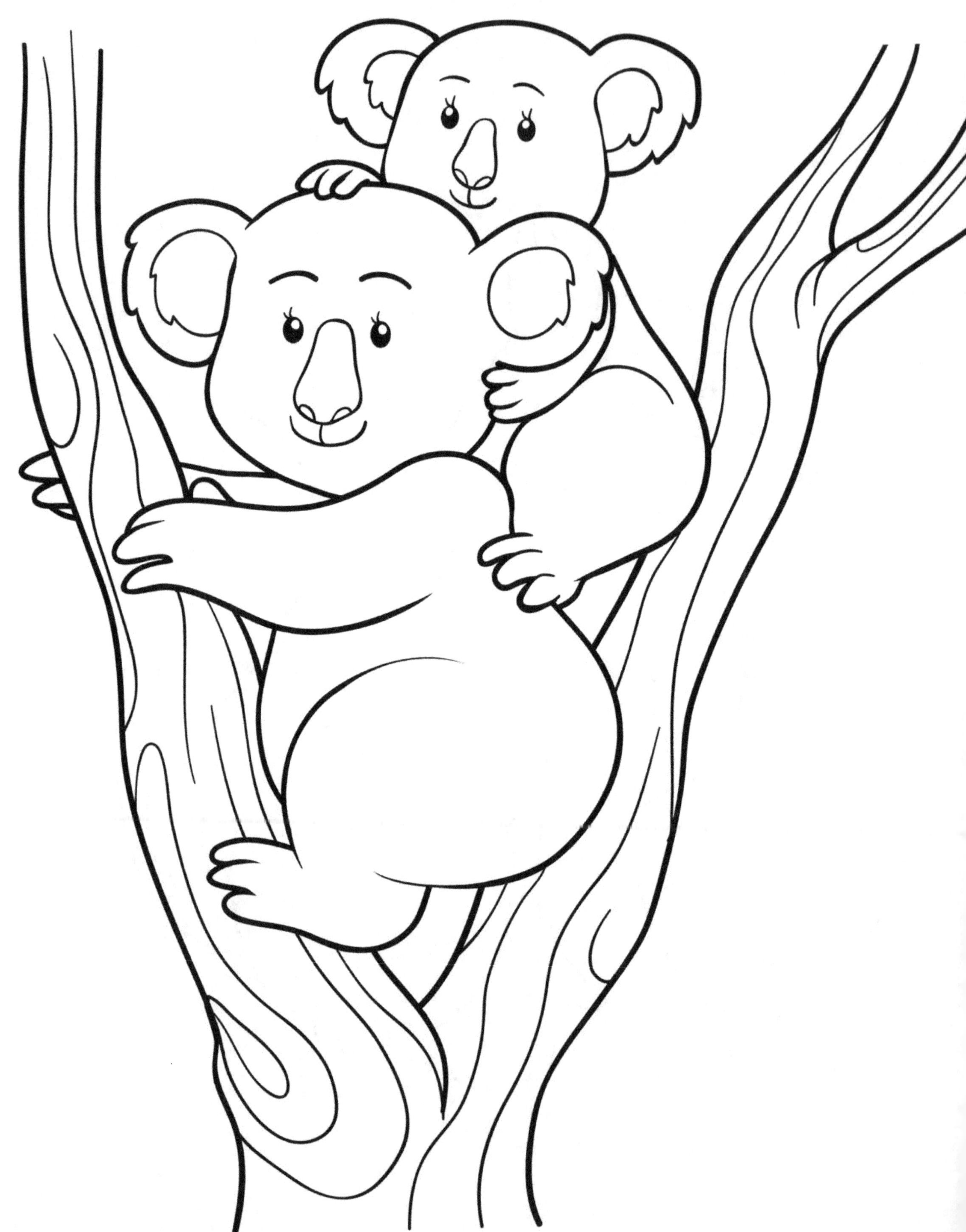

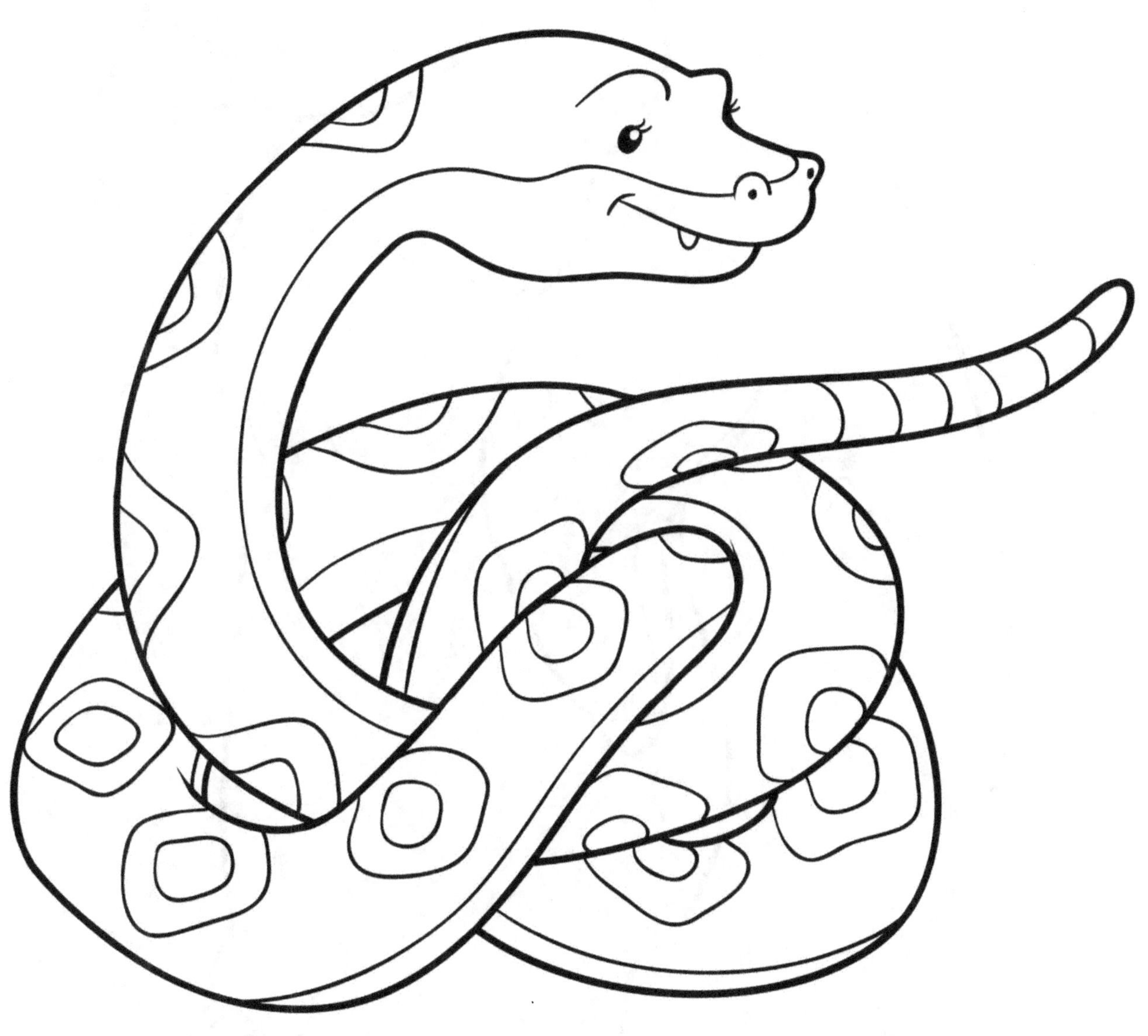

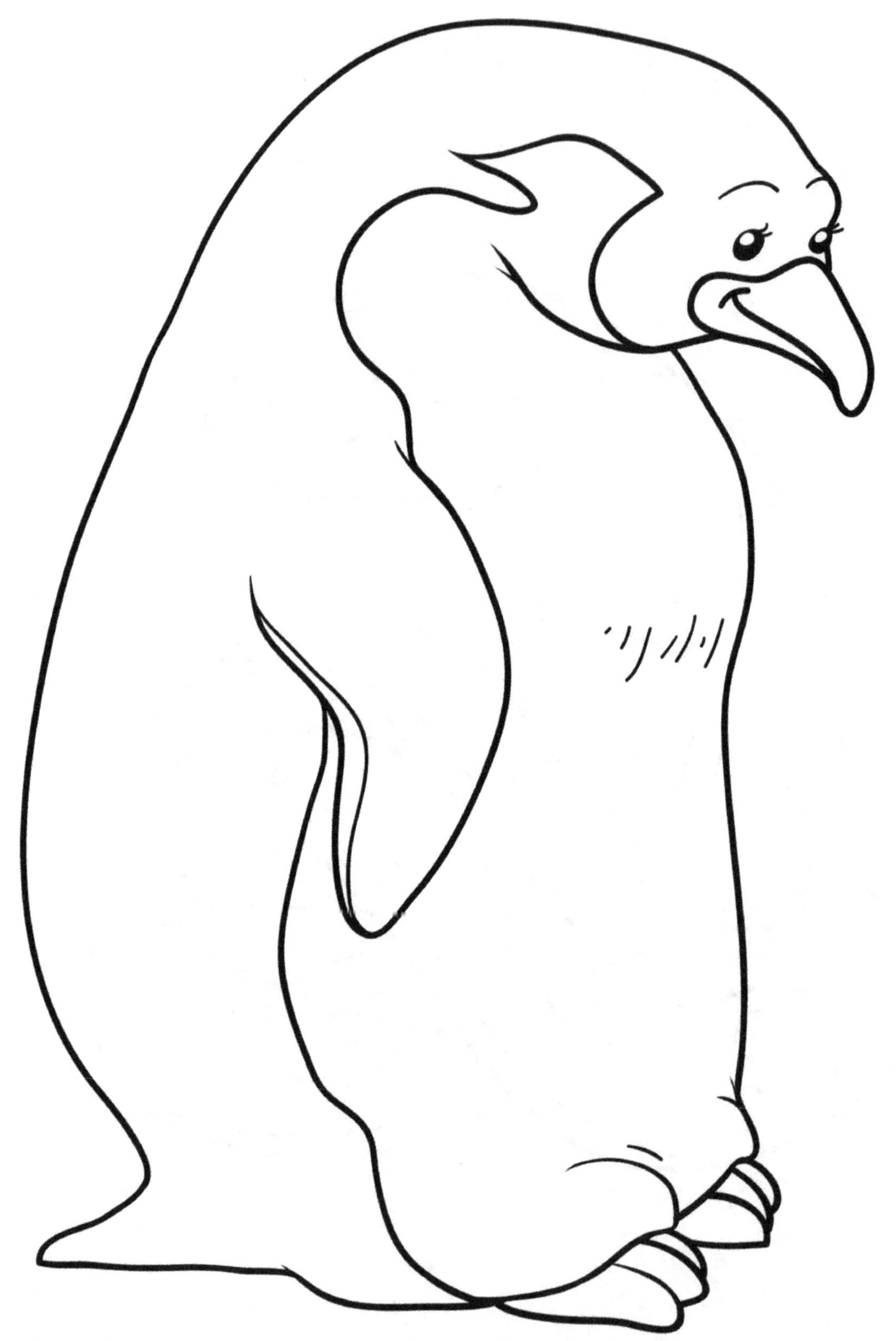

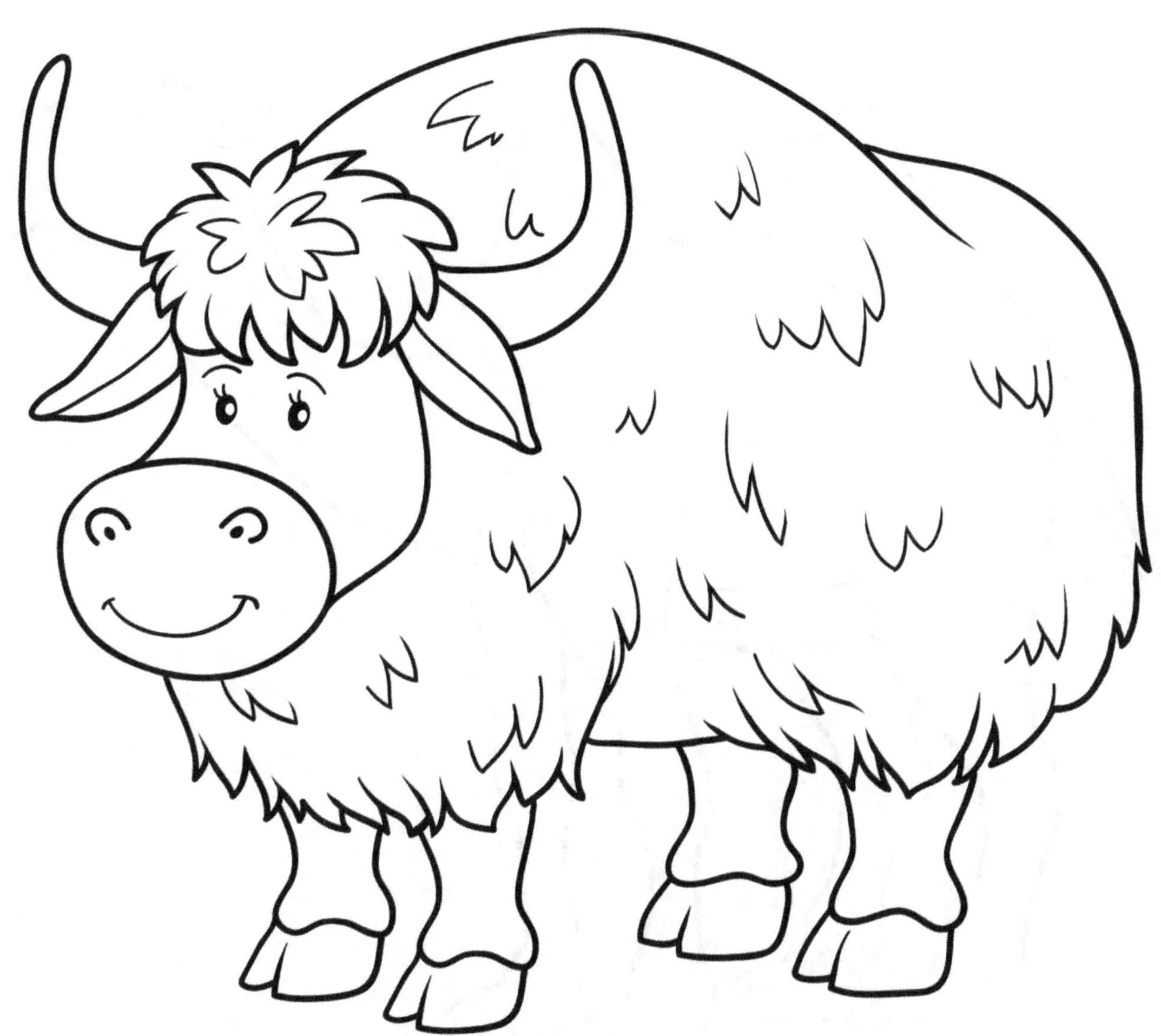

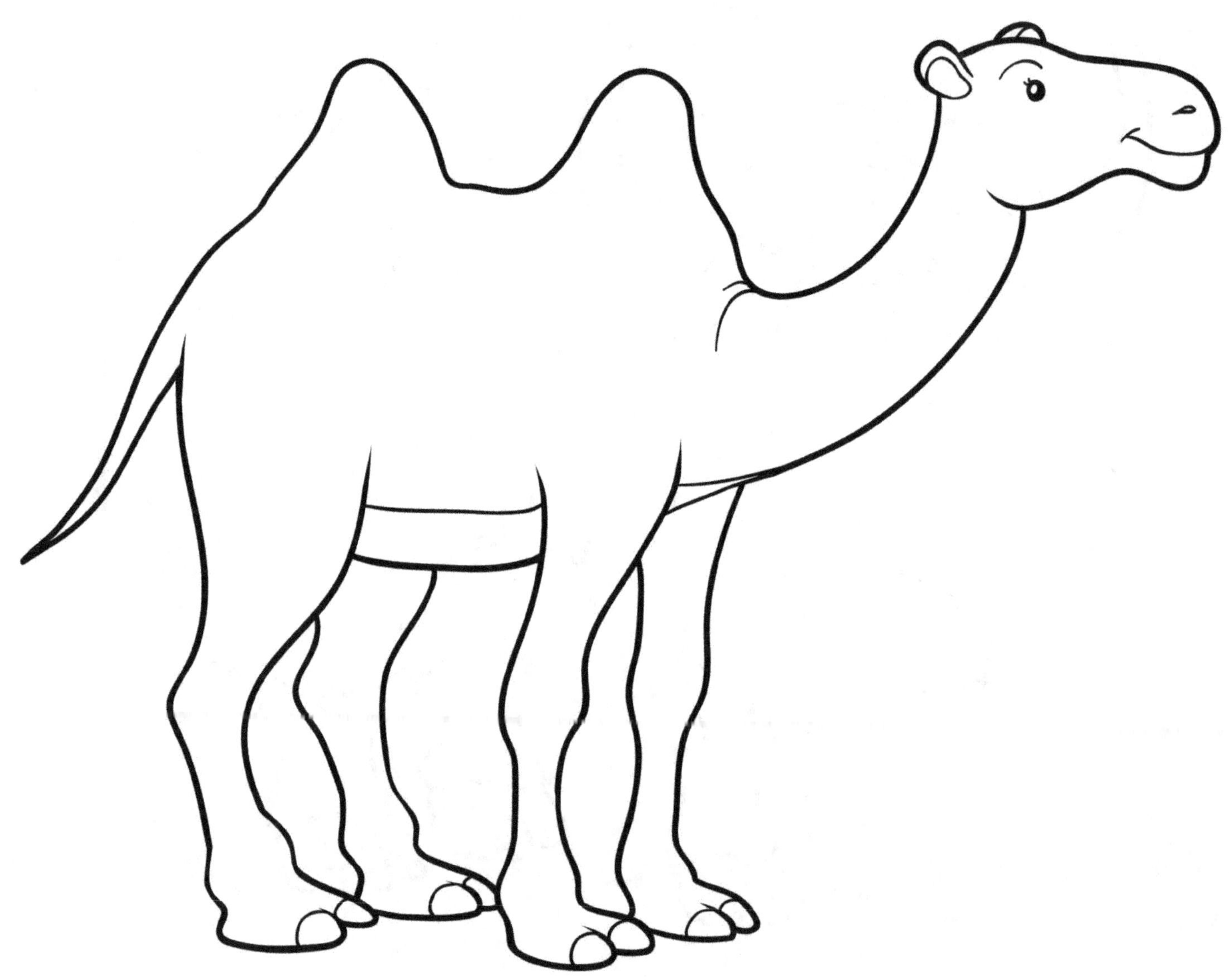

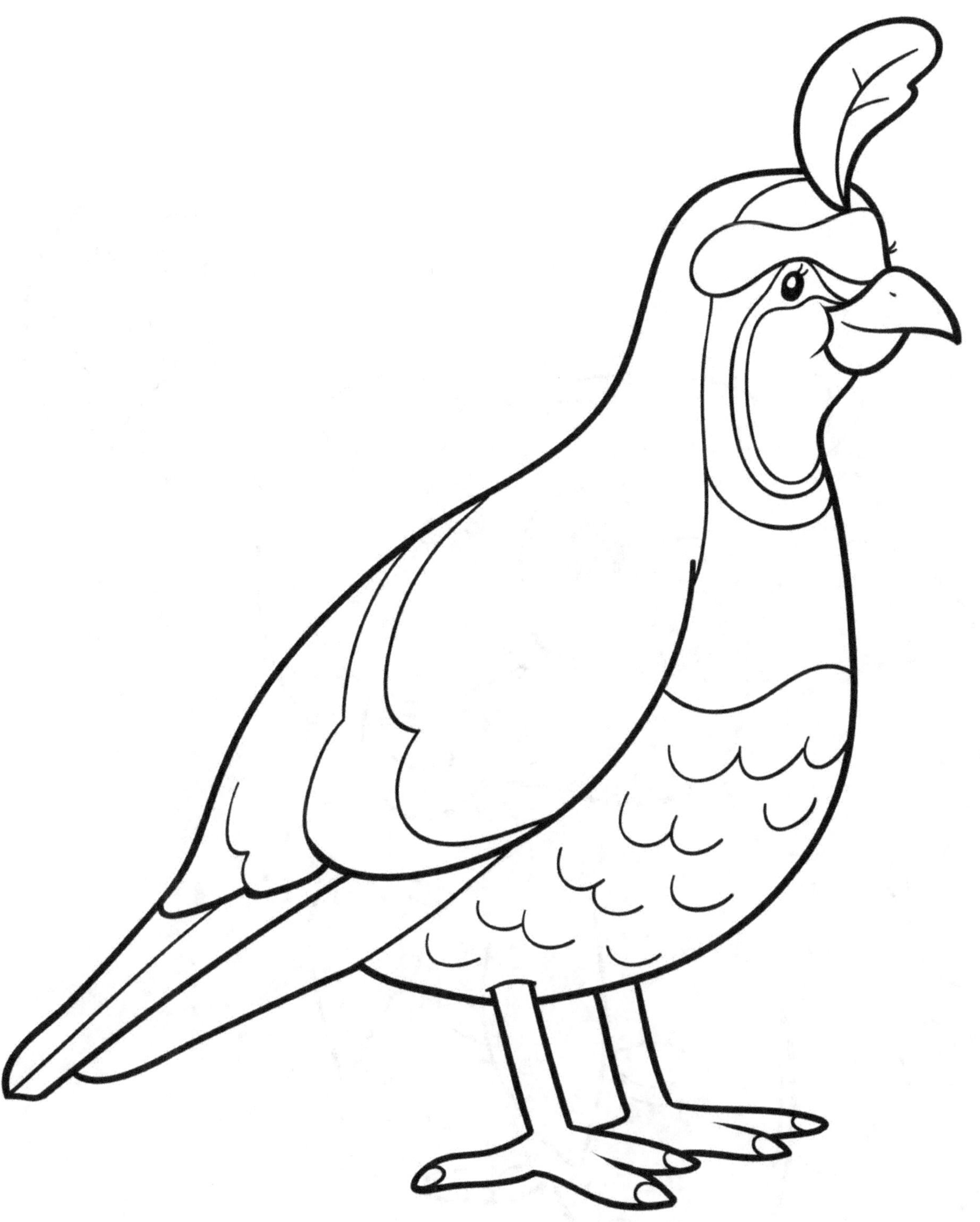

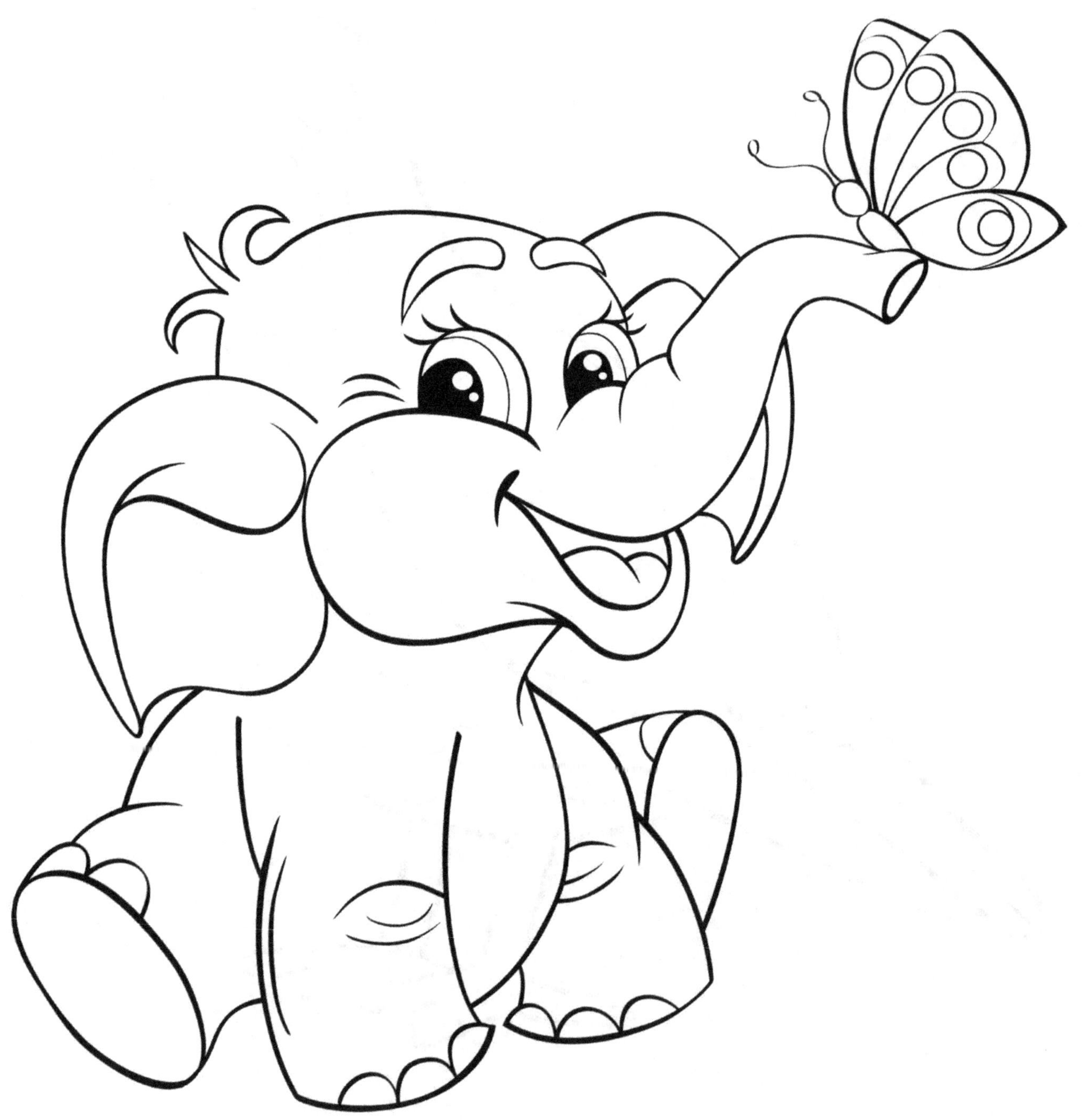

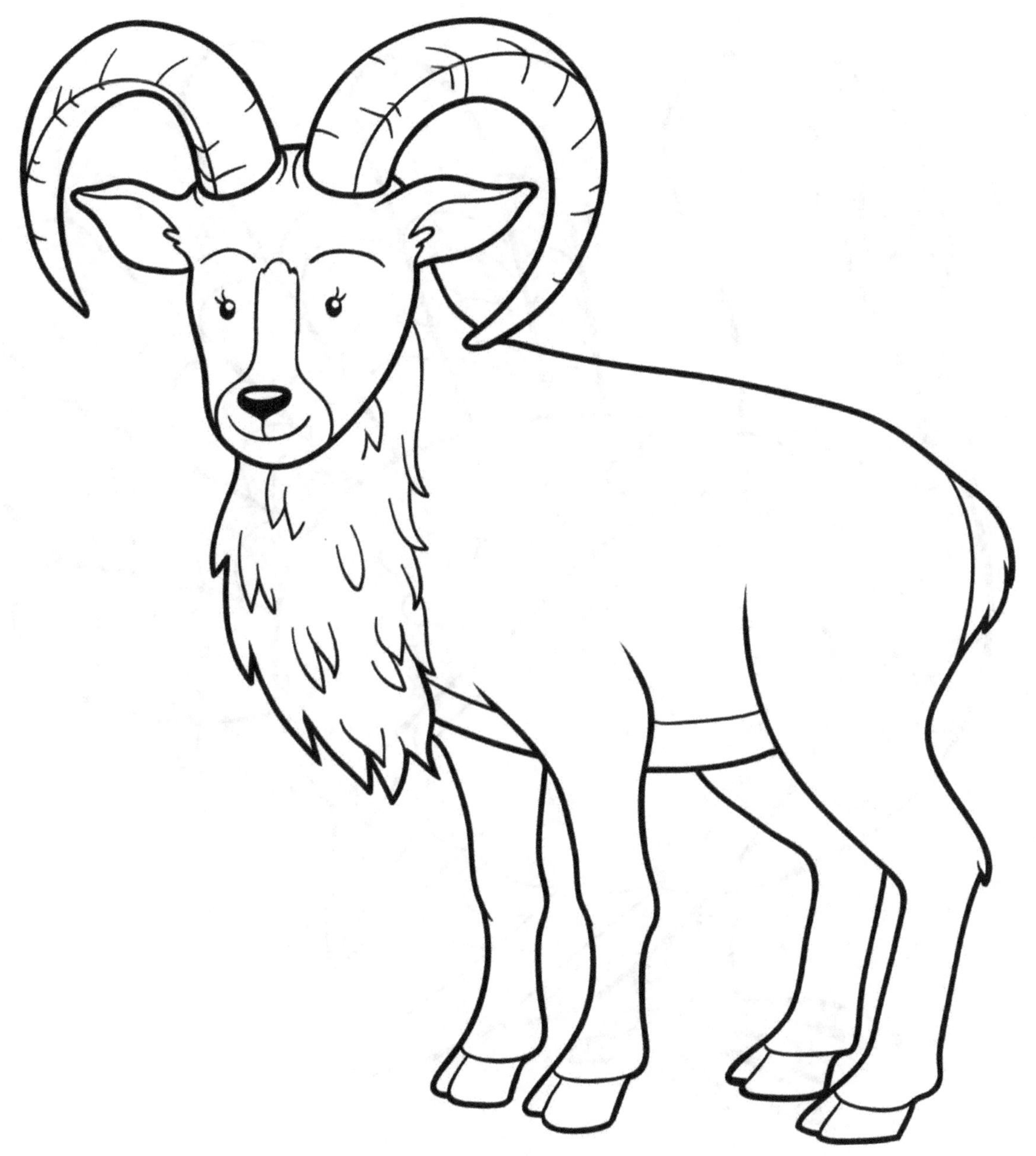

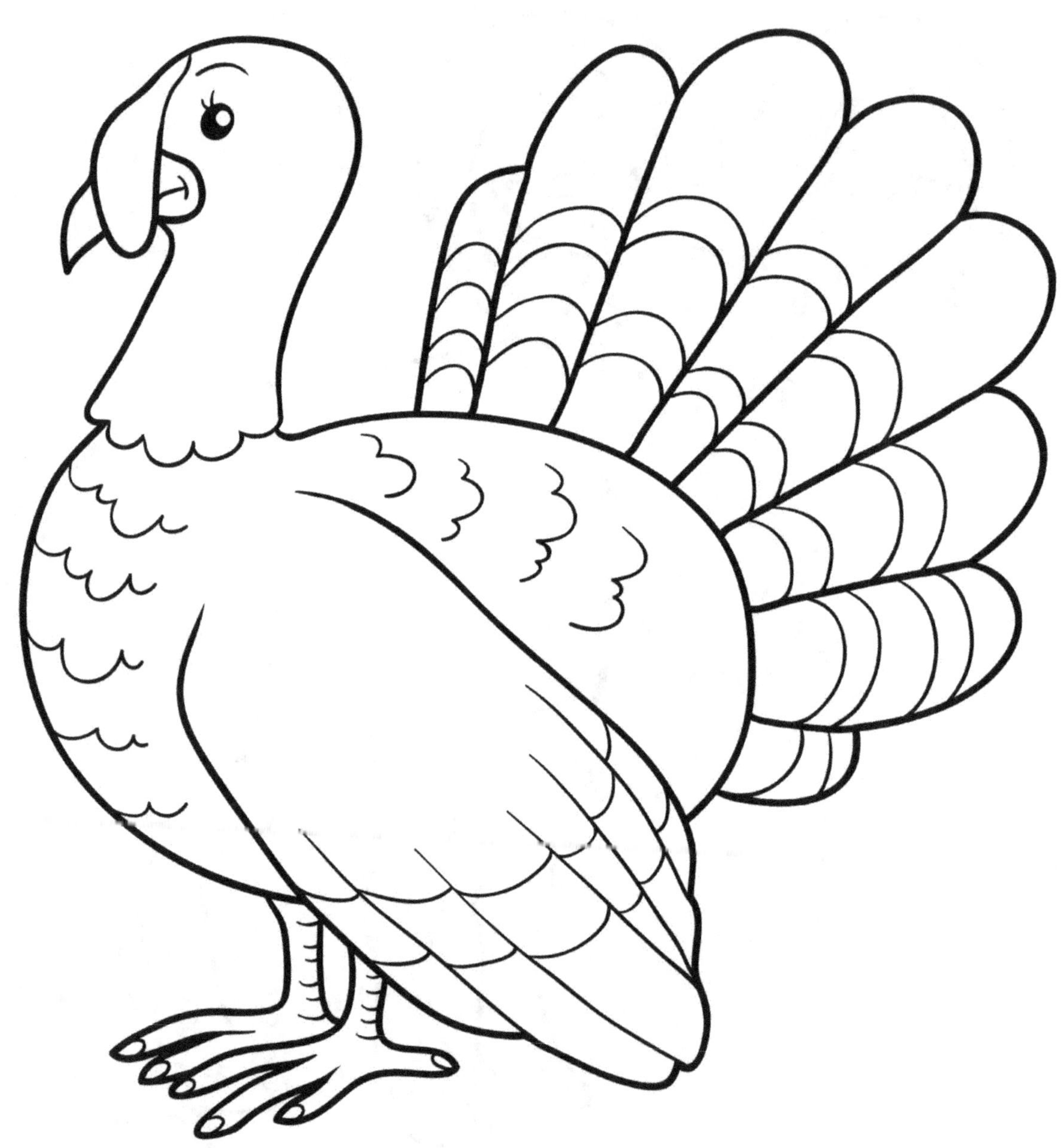

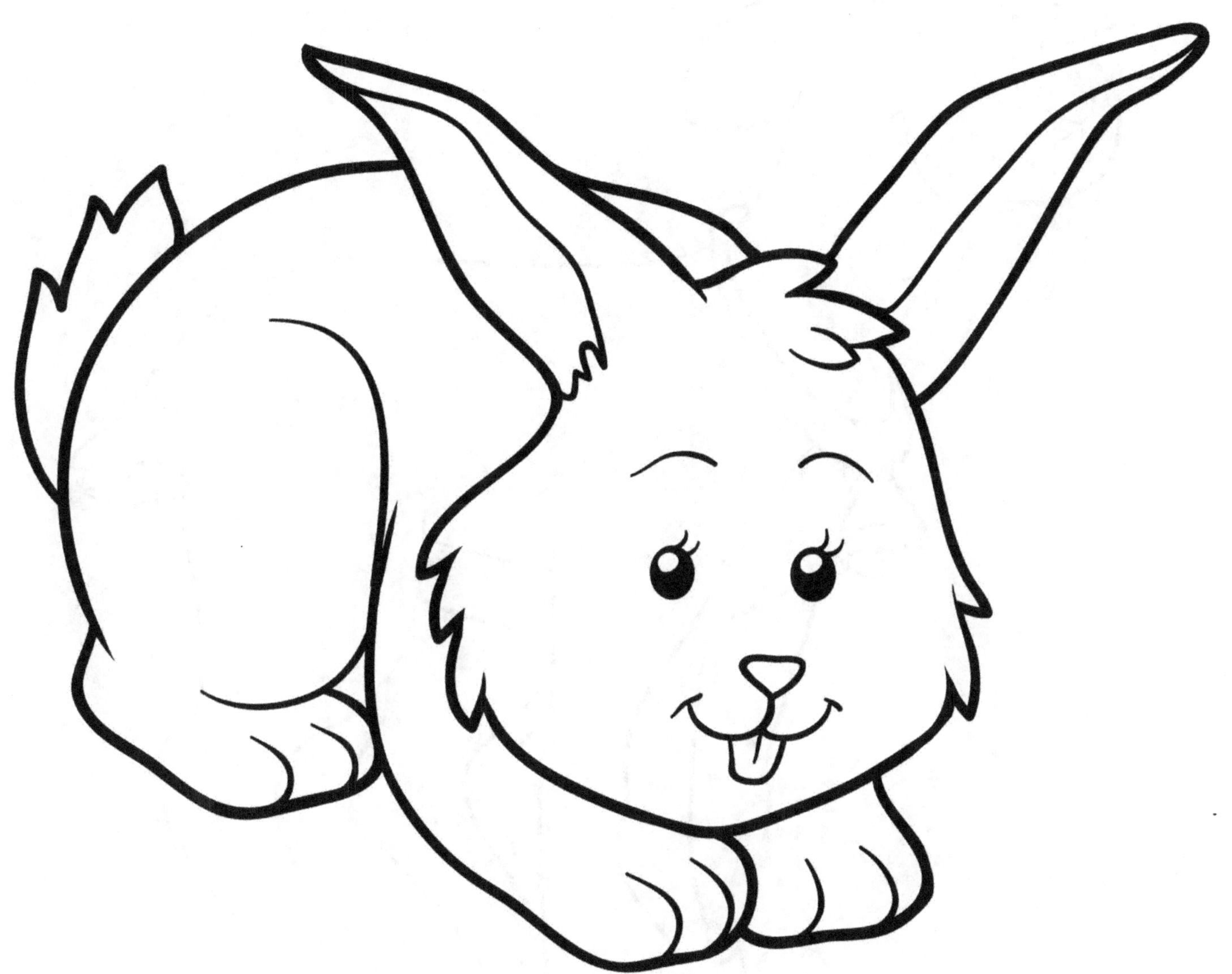

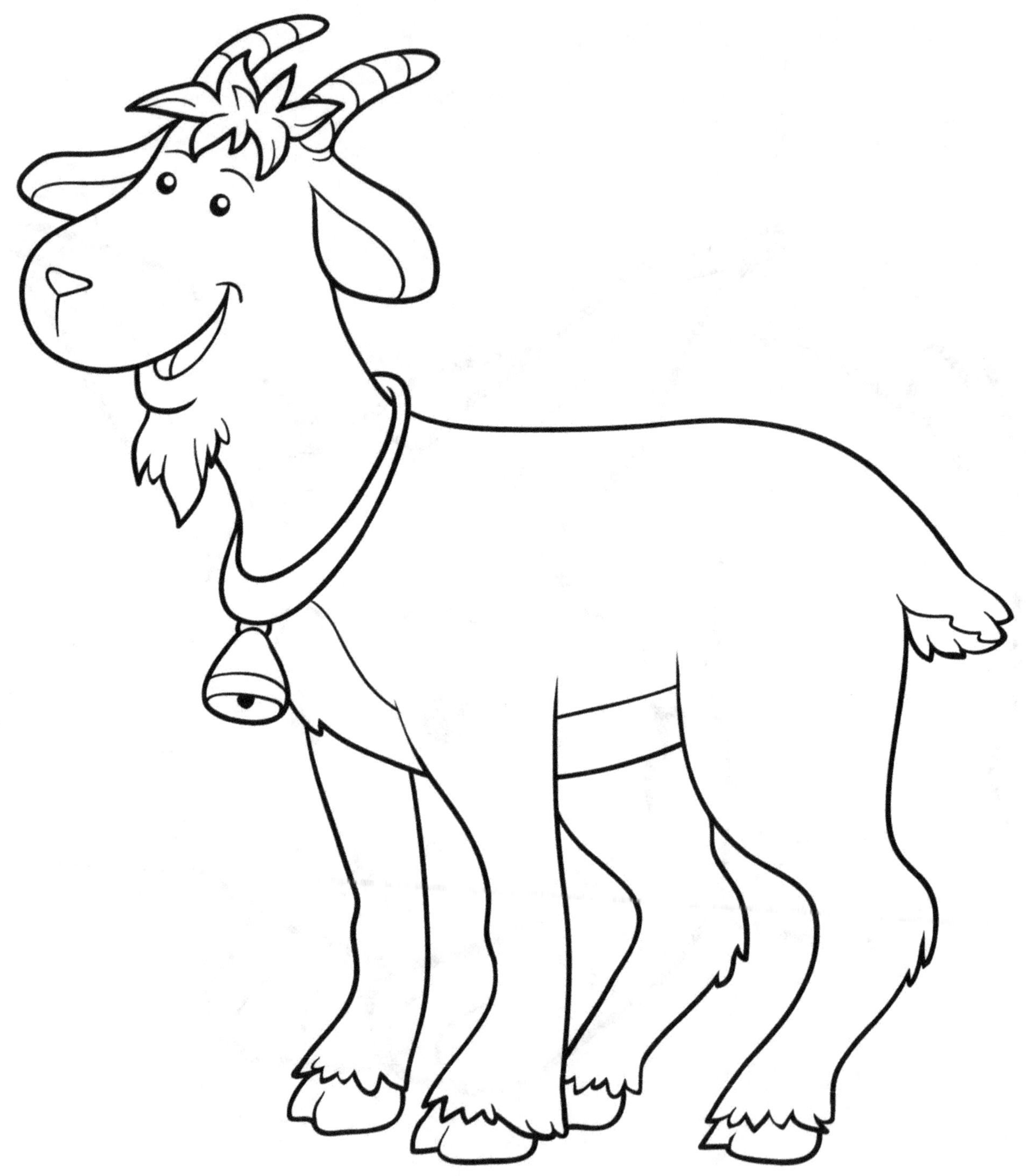

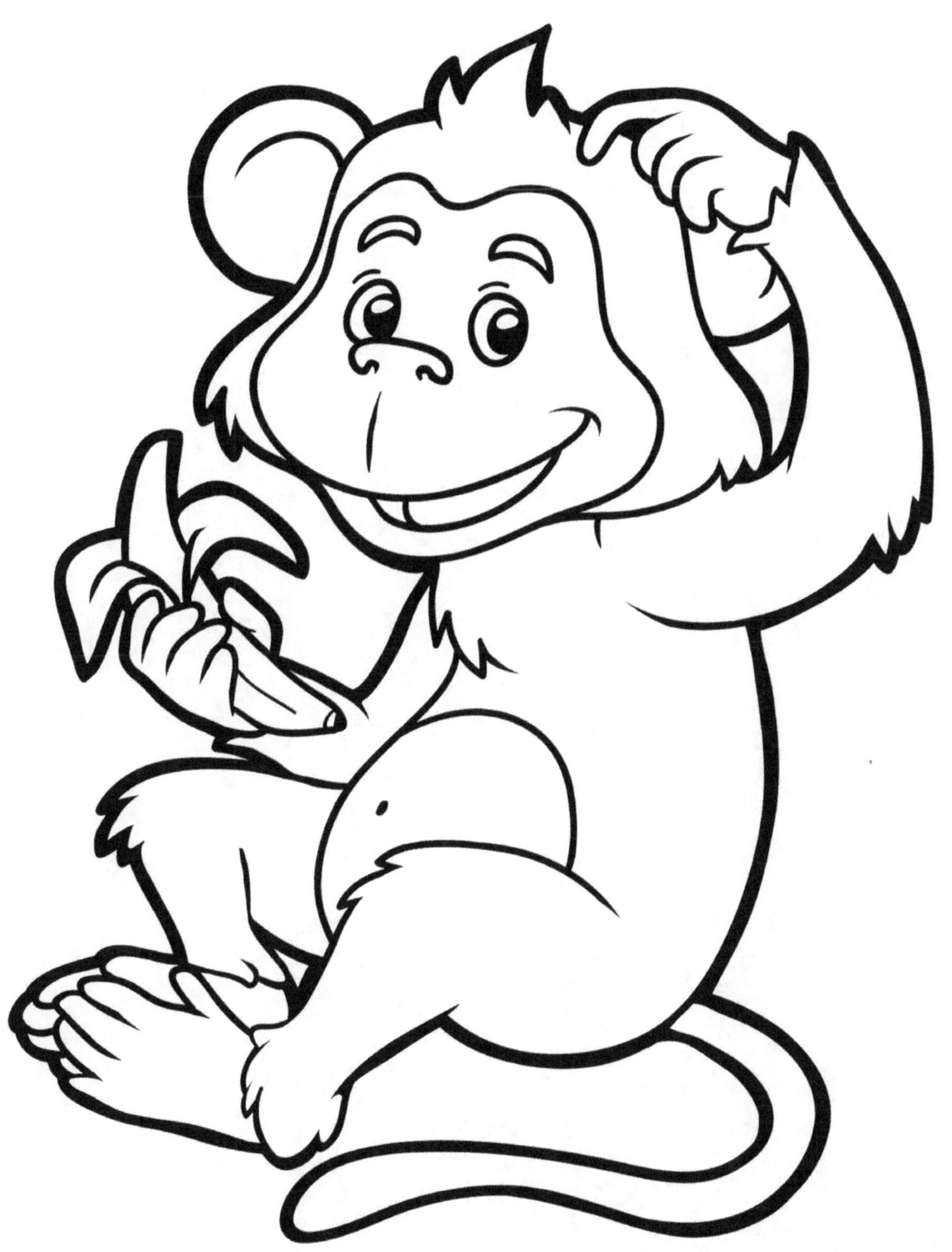